Romans

A Practical Commentary

Brian Poe

CYPRESS

Published by Cypress Publications

Manufactured in the United States of America

Cataloging-in-Publication Data

Poe, Brian, 1982–

Romans

Includes Scripture index.

1. Bible—Romans—Commentaries. I. Poe, Brian Christian, 1982–. II. Title.

227.1077 DDC20

ISBN: 978-1-956811-21-6 (paperback); 978-1-965811-22-3 (ebook).

LCCN: 2023903344

Cover design by Brad McKinnon and Brittany Vander Maas

Cypress Publications
3625 Helton Drive
PO Box HCU
Florence, AL 35630
www.hcu.edu/publications

To my dear late-wife Molly Marie Poe/Decker. She is watching from heaven and I know she would be proud. She once told me that she knew from the start that I loved the Word of God; that was one of the things she fell in love with. That has been a fire in my bones since that day.

Contents

Note From the Author

I have read through many commentaries in my few years of investigating the truths within the Bible. I have found to be true the many complaints I hear from time to time; there are few commentaries available that are easy to use for the average student. I will not mention any commentary sets by name, but most, if not all, seem to swing from one side to the other. Some I have seen are very devotional as they go through the text; they are especially useful for application and understandability, but hardly useful for any academic study to help understand the text. Then the pendulum seems to swing far to the other side; the author goes so deep it leaves the average person bewildered. The average church-goer cannot find a *useful* commentary to use at home unless they are first expected to get a theology degree. That is why it was laid on my heart to write this commentary; I want to reply to the desperate cries for a useable and understandable commentary to aid through the study of God's word. As you go through these pages, you will find the wording to be simple, and the phrasing to be easy to read. Please don't misunderstand me, I am not writing this way to demean you and therefore insult you. I write like this because this is where I am. And I find no need to add larger and more flashy words when it will only impede your understanding and my ability to relay a simple thought. Furthermore, as you read through these pages, you will find the statements and paragraphs to be short and to the point. My purpose is to give you what you need in order to understand the text, but I do not wish to overload you with useless babble. With all that being said, my wish is that you may have a comfortable read through this commentary and will consequently understand the book of Romans in a deeper and fresher way that will strengthen your faith and enrich your walk with the Lord. In the end, may God be given the glory and all honor.

There are several ways a person can go about parsing any given passage; all are beneficial, but most commentators have to pick a method to use. I will note a few, but then I will share how I went about writing this commentary.

Some commentators focus on original language and roots. This provides an intriguing literary guide for some, but not everyone will have much interest or such a need. In this commentary, I only bring in the original language when I thought it necessary to understand the real meaning.

Some commentators are very concise while they delve into every verse. They try to find the substance in every possible thought the writer might have had. These commentaries usually go into history, other resources, context, characters, and so on to give the reader the full picture. These commentaries are like a five-course meal, and for many they are treasures. I attempted to provide a simpler look at this book. I am attempting to find that fine line where you are not given too much, but I don't want to give you too little either.

Some commentators write in a very casual manner and provide a devotional-like book. These commentaries are very heartfelt and help readers on a day-to-day basis, but sometimes they lack depth. While these commentaries are great for many, others want more than a devotional. I attempt to write in a casual manner, but I want to add the depth that one needs to walk away with an understanding of the book of Romans.

So, how did I write this commentary? I wrote it topically, trying to relay the main point of the given passage to the average person in which it was intended when it was first written. This is why I do not want to write for scholars (even if I could), because the letter was not intended for scholars. I want to write to the average person, some Christians, some perhaps not. I want to write at a level that brings understanding. In this commentary, I take a given passage, and I try to sift out the *point* while not getting bogged by the other details that might not matter as much. For an example, take the following statement:

> My wife and I took my boys across the street to go for a bike ride. We made sure we grabbed our phones. I had to tie a wrench to Jesse's bike in case I had to adjust the boy's handlebars. I had to carry the water because Jesse's bike doesn't have a water holder yet. The boys got on their bikes—both are getting too big for them. We are going to have to do something about that soon. But nonetheless, we went on a bike ride. We had a great time. We got home and had a snack.

There are so many ways you could comment on this passage. What do you want your readers to see and understand? What does it mean to you? Do you comment on bike styles or family practices? Maybe you look into tools and bike adjustments. Maybe you could comment on family life in a Christian home. For me, I see a family that enjoyed a bike ride. It seems so simple, but isn't that what happened? This is my approach in the book of Romans.

Brian Poe

Introduction

To begin to understand the text of this letter Paul wrote to the church in Rome, we first must understand a bit of the context and background. Not just that, but in any letter, it is easier to understand the contents if you also know the motivation of the writer. In this brief introduction, we are going to take a small look at the various styles of letters written by Paul. By doing so, we will identify the uniqueness of this particular letter. As in any commentary, we are going to attempt to establish a historical context. Therefore, when we begin to delve into chapter one, you will be aware of important historical details that may render helpful in understanding Paul more adequately. At times, it helps in our studies if we understand not only the writer, but the recipients of the letter. With that being said, we will try to bring clarity to the church in Rome. What would this church have looked like? Not the building, but the people. What kind of people were they? What were their backgrounds? Did they have any religious values? These all play a part in helping us understand why Paul wrote what he wrote. Finally, it is important to try to put ourselves in the mind of Paul and ponder his motivation to write this letter. There must have been a reason; Paul was careful with every action, with every church visited, and with his letter writing. I believe this letter was written with careful thought and with a special purpose and for good reason. As we go through this introduction, I hope to bring these to light. And when we later begin to open chapter one, we will be ready to move forward.

The Nature of Paul's Letter Writing

As most of us have written or received a letter in our time, we can all agree that letters have various styles. I am sorry if you have gotten a *Dear John* letter. They are not the most pleasant to receive, but they get a clear point across. On the other hand, many of us might remember those mushy love letters you wrote to your girlfriend or boyfriend. Some of the better men I know still write such letters to their wives. I would congratulate you if you received an acceptance letter from a college you were trying to get into. Or perhaps you had to write a letter of resignation. There are many more styles that can be listed. But the point is obvious, letters can come in different forms with different motives and intent. The same is true with the letters written by Paul.

I find primarily three genres in which you can categorize the letters of Paul. The first is letters of *personal intent*. What I mean is that the letter was not necessarily written to a congregation, but to an individual. Examples of these letters are First and Second Timothy, Titus, and Philemon. We learn that Paul met Timothy on his second journey. We gather that Timothy became a young preacher and likely worked mostly in Ephesus. Paul, as Timothy's spiritual father, wrote Timothy encouraging words any young preacher would need to read. The same is true of Titus, another young man that Paul had trained and even called a true son in the faith. Titus was caring for the work in Crete that Paul had previously visited. Paul wrote a letter to encourage and strengthen the work. The personal letter Paul wrote to Philemon was much different than the ones written to Timothy and Titus. Philemon was not a minister, but a friend of Paul's. While Paul was in a jail cell, he met Onesimus, a run-a-way slave of Philemon's. Paul led Onesimus to Christ and wrote a letter to Philemon suggesting that he receive him back, not as a slave, but as a brother in Christ. Each of these letters is special and personal to Paul; a one-on-one ministry. This is not the case with the other letters of Paul.

The second style of letter you find Paul to have written is what I call *ministerial follow-up*. Paul went on several missionary journeys as we will see on maps in a few pages. However, after having left a particular church, he would often write to the churches for a variety of reasons. Sometimes, he would hear reports of praise from a church he had previously visited. Such letters were the ones he wrote to the Thessalonians and to the church in Philippi. In these letters, you will not find hardly any reproof to speak of, but mostly words of praise and encouragement. Other follow-up letters Paul wrote were more instructive and even a form of reprimand. These types of letters are what we see when Paul wrote to the churches in Galatia and both letters written to the Corinthians. Paul did not enjoy writing these styles of letters, but he thought it necessary to give instruction to the wayward churches when needed. Not all the letters were praise or reprimand; some were words of encouragement in due time for the struggling churches. We see this form of letter when Paul wrote to the Ephesians and to the Colossians. These letters might also be fitting to be in the letters of praise, but they also have a heavy content of encouraging material to strengthen the church. Regardless of the reason, each of these letters was written to churches Paul had visited, and he wanted to continue to strengthen them in whatever ways he possible.

One final form of letter writing we see from Paul is *a letter written to a church Paul had not yet visited but hopes to visit soon.* This may seem like a lengthy description, but it best describes what we see concerning the letter Paul wrote to the church in Rome. As we survey his journeys, we learn that Paul had never been as far west as Rome. As we learn from his letter, he felt he has done all he could in the regions he had worked for the past few years, and he hoped to go to Spain. His plan was to stop by Rome on his way. As history shows, Paul eventually arrived at Rome, but under quite different circumstances than expected. Paul wrote this letter to the church in Rome to inform them that he would be coming soon. He also wanted to give some instruction on matters pertaining to salvation. We will see these unfold as we get into the letter.

Historical Context

Paul took three journeys as we see detailed in the book of Acts. The purpose of this portion of the introduction is to help plot the letter written to Rome on a timeline. Understanding this brief timeline will help give a full idea of the context of the letter. The three journeys of Paul began about 47 AD and ended in 57 AD. The first journey of

Paul was from 47 AD to 48 AD. We read about this journey in Acts 12:25–14:28. Paul's second journey spanned from 49 AD to 52 AD. We read about this journey in Acts 15:36–18:22. Paul's third journey began about 53 AD and ended in Jerusalem in 57 AD. We read about this journey in Acts 18:23–21:16. It was during Paul's third journey that he wrote his letter to the church in Rome. In Acts 20:1–3, we learn that near the latter part of Paul's third journey, he traveled to Corinth, where he stayed for three months. Furthermore, we learn in Romans 15:19–33 that Paul wrote to the church in Rome that he soon planned to go to Jerusalem in order to deliver the contribution, then he was going to leave for Spain, stopping by Rome on the way. It seems most fitting that Paul was in Corinth during the winter of 56–57 AD. It was during this time that he wrote to the church in Rome. It seems that he had all intention to arrive in Rome later in 58 AD. We know from the book of Acts that this would not happen as planned. Nonetheless, we now have a date to which we can place the letter Paul wrote to the church in Rome.

The Church in Rome

As we read through the letters of Paul, we not only learn the theology and doctrine of Paul, but we also learn a lot about the churches to which he wrote. For instance, the Galatians struggled with works of the law. The Corinthians struggled with immorality. The church in Thessalonica was praised for their behavior and for becoming examples to all believers. I know we are not supposed to pick favorites, but based on Paul's letters, if I were to suggest one of Paul's favorites, it would have been Ephesians. What do we know about the church in Rome from both history and the letter Paul wrote?

There is no strong evidence to help us understand the church's origin. However, Ambrosiaster, a Latin church father of the fourth century, said the Romans "had embraced the faith of Christ, albeit according to the Jewish rite, without seeing any signs of mighty works or any of the apostles." As we get into the letter, we will find this statement to prove itself; Paul made a great effort to show that salvation was not through the law, but through Jesus Christ. Furthermore, Paul made mention a few times how there was no difference between Jew and Gentile while in Christ. What we are going to see when we read through the letter to the Romans is that they did believe in Jesus, but their theology had a lot of Judaism mixed into it that Paul felt he needed to address.

The expulsion by Claudius in 49 AD becomes a big part of our discussion. Prior, to 49 AD, the church in Rome likely consisted of a variety of people, both Jew and Gentile. They likely struggled with their differences, especially those matters pertaining to the law. However, in 49 AD, Claudius commanded all Jews and Christians to leave Rome. This would have left only the Gentile Christians (those who fell just under the government's radar) to maintain the church. There is a likelihood that the church did not meet during those few years, but I suspect some did meet, although being very few in number. During this time, Christians like Aquila and Priscilla would have had to leave Rome and go to Corinth. This is when Paul met them and they joined his ministry; this story is recorded in Acts 18:1–4. The expulsion would have ended at the death of Claudius, which was only a few years later. It is right to assume that when the expulsion ended, many or most of the Jews and Christians would have returned. When Paul wrote to the church in Rome, he asked the church to greet Aquila and Priscilla. There are also quite a number of other Christians Paul mentioned and asked the church to greet. These names will be discussed later, but Paul likely met them throughout Asia and surrounding areas during the expulsion.

With all this being said, we come back to the question of the people in the church in Rome. Paul was a minister to the Gentiles. We will see clearly in the letter that Gentiles were addressed. However, the letter is noticeably written to the Jews as well. The church in Rome was a beautifully diverse group of both Jewish Christians *and* Gentile Christians. However, none of them had a deep understanding of salvation. Furthermore, both groups were stuck in some ideologies from their roots. Paul wrote this letter to unite this diverse church, not in their differences in which some did not matter, but in Christ. Paul wanted them to know, that although, some had a Jewish background, and some a Gentile background, in Christ they could be united.

Why Write a Letter?

I want to return to the basic idea of letter writing and take a moment to look at *motive*. Why did Paul write this letter? The first reason Paul would write this letter to the church in Rome is the *personal connection*. When we get to Romans 16, it is made clear that Paul knew many of the people who had returned to Rome. In fact, many of them he had worked side by side in some way or another. So, Paul would be motivated to write this church to greet many of his co-workers in ministry.

The second reason Paul would write this letter is made evident when considering the zeal Paul had for ministry and changing lives. Paul was very intentional with his visits, where he set up churches, and to whom he wrote letters. Furthermore, with every fiber in his being, he was trying to make the greatest impact possible in the short amount of time he had. With Rome being the center of world power, if Paul could strengthen the church there, the lasting repercussions would be phenomenal. Paul wanted to take advantage of this amazing ministerial opportunity.

The final reason Paul wrote this letter to the church in Rome was to share his intent to visit them soon. As we are going to see in chapter fifteen, Paul planned to travel to Spain. His plans were to stop at Rome on his way. His reason to visit would be to see once again his fellow workers. He would also be able to preach the gospel and strengthen the churches as he did in many other cities. But also, he was hoping to raise funds for his trip, and he was confident that the church in Rome would help.

As a final note, the simple and clear picture is that Paul sent a letter to the church in Rome in the springtime of 57 AD. He wrote and sent this letter from the church in Corinth, where he stayed the winter. Before Paul left, he put the letter in the hands of a courier who would deliver it to the church in Rome. After doing so, Paul left Corinth in the spring, having plans to finish his third missionary journey by going to Jerusalem where he would hand over the funds raised from his campaign. After a quick stop in Jerusalem, Paul planned to head to Rome and embark on a whole new journey to a new part of the world. However, Paul was soon arrested and ended up staying in Jerusalem and Caesarea for about two years. After a couple of years of unresolved debate, Paul appealed to Caesar, and soon after was put on a ship headed to Rome. Paul would get to Rome, but it would be by a quite different plan than his own. The following letter is what Paul wrote to the church prior to his arrival. This letter was life-giving to the Romans, and now some two-thousand years later, there is still life for us if we read with open hearts.

I present to you *Romans*, a letter written by the apostle Paul.

Chapter One

Paul, a servant of Christ Jesus, called to be an apostle and set
apart for the gospel of God. (Rom 1:1 NIV)

P aul began the letter as he did most, by first
introducing himself. This is not a common format
today, but it was the case and very practical in the
ancient world. In many situations, a letter of such length
could be quite long while written on a scroll. In the case of
the letter written to Rome, some believe it could have been as
much as twenty feet long. If you were reading this letter, it
would be inconvenient to have to go to the end of the scroll
to see who the author was. To be practical, and also to set the
authority behind everything that would be heard when being
read to the congregation, Paul would state his identity and
credentials at the very beginning of the letter.

This first verse is rich in what is said about the identity of
Paul. Firstly, Paul identified himself as a *servant of Jesus
Christ*. You can find this similar introduction in Philippians
1:1 and Titus 1:1. There is a distinction that must be made

with words used for *servant* in the writings of Paul. There
were some occasions when Paul spoke of the role of a deacon
in the church, but that is not the word Paul used here. They
are often rendered the same word in English, but the Greek
is different. When Paul called himself a servant in the introduction of Romans, Philippians, and Titus, it is the same
word he used to refer to slaves. Furthermore, the word is
seen again in 1 Corinthians 7:21 and Ephesians 6:5 speaking
of slavery in the clearest way possible. It was this word that
Paul used to refer to his role to the Lord. Paul considered
himself more than just a servant; he literally thought of
himself as a slave unto the Lord. What is the difference? A
servant has rights and perhaps some status. A servant may be
able to come and go and perhaps have ownership of items of
their own. However, a slave is subject to his master in every
way. A slave has no rights. A slave is simply expected to be
obedient. A slave was owned by his master. This was the
view of slavery in the New Testament era. This was how
Paul thought of himself before God. But not out of demand
or coercion; Paul desired to be in full submission to the Lord.
Paul desired to make Jesus his Lord in the fullest respect.

Secondly, as we see in this first verse, Paul identified
himself as an *apostle*. This same introduction can be found
in Paul's letters to the Corinthians, Timothy, and to Titus.
The word apostle, as it is defined in its original language,
literally means, "one sent." This is seen clearly when considering the disciples of Jesus. If you read through the gospels
carefully, you will see that before the disciples are *sent* in
Matthew 10:2 and Mark 6:30, they were always called disciples, which is a student or pupil. However, after they are
literally sent by Jesus to do good works and evangelism, they
were also called apostles—ones sent. Paul understood his

ministry and that it was not merely a vocation that he chose. Paul knew clearly that he was sent by God to be a minister to the Gentiles (also see Rom 10:14–15 and 15:14–16). When considering only these first two roles ascribed to Paul, as being a slave and one sent, it is clear that Paul's ministry was not something Paul thought he chose to do; it was what he felt he had to do, it was what brought meaning, it was his purpose.

The third identity we see Paul speak of himself is that he was *set apart* for the gospel. This is a peculiar word, and if only taken at English face value, some nuance may be missed. One might quickly think of the word *holiness*, for it also means to be set apart. If this word was the same in Greek, the English translators would most assuredly insert "holiness," in Romans 1:1 rather than "set apart." However, Paul used a different word. The word Paul used here in this introduction speaks of a very physical idea of being severed, divided, or separated even by a boundary. Furthermore, Paul added that he was set apart *for the gospel*. In the mindset of Paul, he was set apart to preach the gospel. It was *not* merely something he did amongst other things; it was the very core of why he took every breath. In fact, his life that we read about, and this verse, reveals that it was the *only* thing he lived for. Paul had severed himself from all worldly distractions to do this one thing he was sent by God to do. When Paul wrote, "for me to live is Christ," this is what he meant to the fullest degree. With every breath Paul took, it was going to be for Christ. All other things would be set aside.

When the letter to the church in Rome was opened up and read before the congregation, these were the first few words that would have been uttered. The people would immediately understand who wrote the letter. But moreover, and most importantly, they would understand that this letter was written with no personal agenda of a mere man, but a man who was in full surrender to the Lord—one sent by God. The people would have seen that Paul had separated himself from all worldly distractions to only preach the Word of God with zeal, and with that same zeal, this letter was penned. This would have set the tone and the authority. This would have drawn their attention to listen and learn about their great salvation that Paul would clearly lay out before them on the pages to follow.

> The gospel He promised beforehand through His prophets in the Holy Scriptures regarding His Son, who as to His earthly life was a descendant of David, and who through the Spirit of holiness was appointed the Son of God in power by His resurrection from the dead: Jesus Christ our Lord. Through Him we received grace and apostleship to call all the Gentiles to the obedience that comes from faith for His name's sake. And you also are among those Gentiles who are called to belong to Jesus Christ. To all in Rome who are loved by God and called to be His holy people: Grace and peace to you from God our Father and from the Lord Jesus Christ (Rom 1:2–7).

We discussed briefly in the introduction the identity of the people in which Paul was writing. The conclusion was made that Paul was writing to both the Christian Jew *and* the Christian Gentile. In this portion of Paul's introduction, we see that to be true. This would also explain why Paul addresses both Jew and Gentile in Romans 2:14 and 17, and in fact, throughout the whole letter. Romans was evidently written to both groups, even as diverse as they often were.

Paul adequately spoke to both with a perfect balance in this one letter. If there was any letter of Paul's that would speak toward the equality of Jew and Gentile while in Christ, it would be this one letter Paul wrote to the Romans.

Paul began with a powerful and yet brilliant statement to connect the Jew and Gentile theologically. By Paul's mention of the *gospel*, he immediately attracted the Gentiles who were more accepting of the new language ushered in by the New Covenant. The gospel was the good news of Jesus Christ. Yet, Paul said the gospel was that which was *promised beforehand through [the] prophets*. This would be an immediate attraction to the Jew. The Jews were not wanting to give up their holy writings. Paul was revealing that in order to be a part of the gospel, one did not have to give up the Jewish Scriptures; the two are in one. And as we delve into the chapters of this letter, we will see Paul make good use of the *Holy Scriptures* while speaking of the gospel of Jesus Christ.

It has long been debated the relationship between the Old and New Testaments. There was much animosity, especially in the first few centuries of the church. The difficulty was in what to do with the Jewish Scriptures (Old Testament) while trying to move forward with the new. Many in the early centuries thought that a Christian must disregard the Old Testament, and some also thought that the God of the Old Testament was an evil God. Even today, there are many who disregard the Old Testament and add that there are no Old Testament prophecies of Christ. I can go to many Scriptures to embrace the truth I am presenting, but this verse we are looking at alone gives us an appropriate answer; the gospel was promised from the prophets of old. This simply says that Jesus was foretold by the writers spoken of in the Old Testament. When Paul wrote to the Galatians, he spoke of the law as a schoolmaster, or a guardian (Gal 3:24). It is clear from Paul's point of view that the Old Testament was not only useful but it foretold of Jesus. Paul phrases this introduction in such a way as to allow both the Gentile and the Jew to come to a common ground in salvation. We will see this point amplified in later verses; salvation is for all.

A final point must be made before we move on. Paul spoke of *obedience that comes from faith* while he spoke of salvation. We will see this unfold more clearly in the letter, but we must understand that in Paul's mind, faith was not the end, but the beginning—faith produces. From this passage, Paul spoke of obedience that is produced by one's faith. Scripture clearly shows that it was this obedience that leads to salvation. Yes, it begins with faith, and therefore, one can say they were saved by faith. But faith was only where the road started—salvation was the end—obedience was the means. At this point, we are left with only one question: what is the *obedience* Paul was speaking of that leads to salvation? We will see this question answer itself as the letter continues.

> First, I thank my God through Jesus Christ for all of you, because your faith is being reported all over the world. God, whom I serve in my spirit in preaching the gospel of His Son, is my witness how constantly I remember you in my prayers at all times; and I pray that now at last by God's will the way may be opened for me to come to you. I long to see you so that I may impart to you some spiritual gift to make you strong—that is, that you and I may be mutually encouraged by each other's faith. I do not want you to be unaware, brothers and sisters, that I

planned many times to come to you (but have been prevented from doing so until now) in order that I might have a harvest among you, just as I have had among the other Gentiles. I am obligated both to Greeks and non-Greeks, both to the wise and the foolish. That is why I am so eager to preach the gospel also to you who are in Rome. For I am not ashamed of the gospel, because it is the power of God that brings salvation to everyone who believes: first to the Jew, then to the Gentile. For in the gospel the righteousness of God is revealed—a righteousness that is by faith from first to last, just as it is written: "The righteous will live by faith" (Rom 1:8–17).

Paul was attempting to connect with his audience. By doing so, he began with words of praise. He was not using flattery, but genuine praise from reports that he had heard. An often-effective way to attract people's attention is to make them feel that the dialogue is somewhat about them. Early in the letter, Paul wanted the people to feel connected and thought of. Paul wanted them to know that their hard work was not overlooked. He now had their attention, now it was time to get to the meat of the letter.

Furthermore, Paul took this time to tell them about his desire to go to Rome. He wanted to go to Rome because he had an obligation to preach to all people. He wrote that he desired to impart spiritual gifts to strengthen the church. However, he had been prevented up to this time. He asked them to pray that the door might be opened to finally come.

I want to take a closer look now at verses 14–17 so that we might understand the depth of what Paul was saying. Paul was a zealot, and he felt obligated to preach to all nations. As I mentioned before, it was for this reason that he wanted to go to Rome. Now if we move forward to verse 16, Paul said he was not ashamed. The reason Paul was not ashamed was he was persuaded that it was what he was called to do. Furthermore, he knew that preaching the gospel was for the purpose of the salvation of many. And Paul refused to let his own pride stand in the way of others coming to Christ.

Paul mentioned that salvation was for the Jew first and then for the Gentile. While this verse has stirred much debate and confusion, I believe it is quite simple. It is not speaking of priority or one being more important than the other. We are going to speak of this in greater depth in chapter eleven, but for now, I will give a simple overview. The Jews were already offered salvation and the blessings of God. Furthermore, the Messiah was promised to the Jews long ago. They were always meant to be part of the plan. But we know that the Jews rejected the salvation of God, causing God to turn to the Gentiles and offer the same salvation to them. I want to be clear; God was not blindsided. God had always planned to offer salvation to the whole world. But if you were to literally play this out on a timeline, salvation was offered to the Jew first, and then to the Gentile. However, the point is clear—salvation is for all.

> The wrath of God is being revealed from heaven against all the godlessness and wickedness of people, who suppress the truth by their wickedness, since what may be known about God is plain to them, because God has made it plain to them. For since the creation of the world God's invisible qualities—His eternal power and divine nature—have been clearly seen, being understood from what has been made, so that people are without excuse.

For although they knew God, they neither glorified Him as God nor gave thanks to Him, but their thinking became futile and their foolish hearts were darkened. Although they claimed to be wise, they became fools and exchanged the glory of the immortal God for images made to look like a mortal human being and birds and animals and reptiles. Therefore God gave them over in the sinful desires of their hearts to sexual impurity for the degrading of their bodies with one another. They exchanged the truth about God for a lie, and worshiped and served created things rather than the Creator—who is forever praised. Amen. Because of this, God gave them over to shameful lusts. Even their women exchanged natural sexual relations for unnatural ones. In the same way the men also abandoned natural relations with women and were inflamed with lust for one another. Men committed shameful acts with other men, and received in themselves the due penalty for their error. Furthermore, just as they did not think it worthwhile to retain the knowledge of God, so God gave them over to a depraved mind, so that they do what ought not to be done. They have become filled with every kind of wickedness, evil, greed and depravity. They are full of envy, murder, strife, deceit and malice. They are gossips, slanderers, God-haters, insolent, arrogant and boastful; they invent ways of doing evil; they disobey their parents; they have no understanding, no fidelity, no love, no mercy. Although they know God's righteous decree that those who do such things deserve death, they not only continue to do these very things but also approve of those who practice them (Rom 1:18–32).

I understand that these verses can be parsed in much greater detail than what I am going to do for you. But my intent is not to get bogged down with each verse to the point of missing the main point. The point we must see is that God's wrath had been kindled. Why? Because of sin.

This is the beginning of a case that Paul was about to begin building; not against the Romans only, but against all of humanity and their perpetual sin. Paul started the case in 1:18, and we will see the case play out until 3:20. Paul's point was to reveal the sinful nature of all men and women.

Paul began to speak of the sin of those in the world; those outside of the church and outside of Judaism. Paul clarified that even those who had never heard or read the Scriptures were accountable for their sin; they had been clearly shown the ways of God in the creation. Now as the church in Rome would hear this portion being read, they would be in complete agreement. They clearly understood the sin of the world and its pending judgment. But what they did not know was that Paul was setting them up. Chapter two is going to bring them into the same category as the world—sinners. That is really as simple as this passage is; it is the beginning of Paul's case showing them that *all* are lost in sin outside of the mercies of Christ. Why is this important to know? It is only when people first realize they are lost in sin that they come to understand the need for a savior.

Chapter Two

Paul ended chapter one by addressing the pagan world (those outside the church). His objective was to point out that although some may have never heard the Scriptures, they were still responsible for the penalty of sin because they were given proof in creation. There seem to be two primary reasons for Paul to bring this up: first, Paul was beginning to build the case that all humanity was lost in sin and was therefore in need of a savior; secondly, Paul was strategically setting the church up to receive the message of salvation. The key is that before people will ever respond to a savior, they must first know they are sinners and in need of forgiveness.

When this letter was read in the hearing of the congregation, they would have heard what Paul wrote about those in the world, and they couldn't have agreed more—the world was full of sin. Some of them most likely thought themselves better than the world. They were, after all, the church. *The church definitely did not sin like the world sinned*—they would have thought in their self-righteousness. They were about to be awakened as they began to hear the content of chapter two.

> You, therefore, have no excuse, you who pass judgment on someone else, for at whatever point you judge another, you are condemning yourself, because you who pass judgment do the same things. Now we know that God's judgment against those who do such things is based on truth. So when you, a mere human being, pass judgment on them and yet do the same things, do you think you will escape God's judgment? Or do you show contempt for the riches of His kindness, forbearance and patience, not realizing that God's kindness is intended to lead you to repentance? But because of your stubbornness and your unrepentant heart, you are storing up wrath against yourself for the day of God's wrath, when His righteous judgment will be revealed. God "will repay each person according to what they have done." To those who by persistence in doing good seek glory, honor and immortality, He will give eternal life. But for those who are self-seeking and who reject the truth and follow evil, there will be wrath and anger. There will be trouble and distress for every human being who does evil: first for the Jew, then for the Gentile; but glory, honor and peace for everyone who does good: first for the Jew, then for the Gentile. For God does not show favoritism (Rom 2:1–11).

Once again, the picture we have here is that the church would have stumbled into looking at the fallacy of the world in judgment and thought two things: First, they would have been quite aware of how sinful the world was, but not with an attitude of love or concern, but judgment; second, they would have had the selfish notion that they were better. By comparing themselves with the world, they would have not only seen the world as the sinners that they were but would have justified *their own* sin that seemed to be much less severe. However, Paul responded by telling them they are guilty of the same sin as the world. He did not mean it was literally the same sin, for in Paul's mind, sin was sin. And that was the very point Paul was trying to make; the world sinned, the Christians sinned, and neither sin is any better. All sin needed to be atoned for.

In verse 4, Paul spoke of showing *contempt for the riches of His kindness, forbearance and patience*. This is what happens when people feel they have been good enough to earn their own salvation. In this scenario, Paul was likely reflecting on the Jewish Christians in the church who not only would have looked quite righteous compared to most everyone else, but they also knew that they were true descendants of Abraham. The Jews took great pride in their heritage, and for some, they felt that their ancestry was enough to earn the gifts of God. Paul is going to deal with this in greater detail in chapter nine. For now, Paul was trying to get the attention of the Christians in the church; they were more concerned with self–exaltation and looking down on the outside sinners rather than sharing the primary concern of God—sharing His love with every soul.

This problem did not only exist between the church and the world; a judgmental attitude will show no boundaries. I have shared the problem of the church judging the world, but I believe the church would have had issues even within its walls. The church in Rome was comprised of both Jews and Gentiles, two groups that were not always easily reconcilable. The Gentiles would have judged the Jews for their old-fashioned practices. The Jews would have certainly judged the Gentiles for their disregard for the law and other Old Testament customs. Paul was trying to address their hearts; he wanted to teach them to see each other through the eyes of Christ.

I would like to go a little deeper with this topic before we move on—what causes a person to become judgmental, or in what ways does a person usually judge another? I think one reason some may judge others is they themselves have lived a good life and they take pride in it. The church was not exempt from this attitude. Another reason a person might judge another is because of heritage. If a person was raised in the right family, or brought up in the right church, that could turn into pride as they look at those who had not. People can become judgmental if they think they are right and the other person is wrong. But even if people are wrong, how they handle the situation is telling of their character—Jesus was always right, but never possessed a judgmental attitude. Lastly, I believe judging can be a means of deflecting. When people put so much attention on the sin and downfalls of others, it puts less or no attention on their own sins. It really all comes back to the heart.

The key problem, and really the only problem Paul addressed in this church was the idea that the church had become judgmental over those around them while sitting in their lofty seats thinking they were better by their own merits. While they did this, they would dismiss their own sins, after all, their sins were not half as bad as the sins of the world around them. There are a few lessons we need to take from this: First, we need to understand the destructive force of sin, no matter what the size of the sin. The fact is, it is usually the *small* sins that cause the most damage as they are often dismissed and left unattended; secondly, we need to understand that it is not our place to sit around and judge. There is no such verse giving any command to do so. The Pharisees thought it was their responsibility—they were wrong. Lastly, we must understand that the *only* reason we have the salvation that we are comfortably enjoying right now is because of the kindness of God. We did nothing to earn or deserve it. And it is important to constantly remember that God desires to pour that same kindness out on the whole world.

When we look at people, when we see them, and when we think about them, it is imperative that we first think of what God sees. God sees a person whom He loves and desires to be part of His kingdom. When Jesus was on the earth, everything He said and every action pointed toward the salvation of all men and women. What do you see when you look at others?

All who sin apart from the law will also perish apart from the law, and all who sin under the law will be judged by the law. For it is not those who hear the law who are righteous in God's sight, but it is those who obey the law who will be declared righteous. (Indeed, when Gentiles, who do not have the law, do by nature things required by the law, they are a law for themselves, even though they do not have the law. They show that the requirements of the law are written on their hearts, their consciences also bearing witness, and their thoughts sometimes accusing them and at other times even defending them.) This will take place on the day when God judges people's secrets through Jesus Christ, as my gospel declares (Rom 2:12–16).

What is fascinating is that Paul did not ask the Gentiles to come under the law of Moses; however, he made it clear by mentioning that they were not free to do whatever they wanted. The Gentiles in Rome probably had never read the law. In chapter three, Paul asked a hypothetical question that he immediately answered; what advantage was it to be a Jew? His answer in part was that they were given the law. Paul agreed that it was an advantage to having the law given to you. However, the Gentiles did not have such an advantage.

The Gentiles were not under the law of Moses, but Paul introduced the law of one's conscience. He was building on the point he began in chapter one; simply said, there are some things in life that people *know* are right and wrong. A clear example would be the case of murder. A person does not have to read it in a law book to know that murder is wrong. It is ingrained in the conscience of a person. Are there some that have medical conditions or seared consciences? Yes, of course. But I think we will agree that the average person has a basic concept of right and wrong notwithstanding the law of Moses.

Paul was attempting to meet the Gentiles *where they were*. Remember the point of this section is that Paul was beginning to build a case that all are sinners. It would be fruitless to pose the Gentile against the law of Moses. They would have quickly rejected that. But there had to be some responsibility to hold them accountable. The Gentiles would have been more acquainted with Greek philosophy which was strong on the human conscience. Rather than Paul rejecting that way of thinking, he meets the Gentles there. Paul had one objective at this time; he wanted to set them up to see the need for a savior. The purpose of this section was to show the Gentiles that even they were under a law, not the law of Moses, but the law of conscience. If there was law, there was responsibility. If there was law, there was sin. Paul had them right where he wanted them.

> Now you, if you call yourself a Jew; if you rely on the law and boast in God; if you know His will and approve of what is superior because you are instructed by the law; if you are convinced that you are a guide for the blind, a light for those who are in the dark, an instructor of the foolish, a teacher of little children, because you have in the law the embodiment of knowledge and truth—you, then, who teach others, do you not teach yourself? You who preach against stealing, do you steal? You who say that people should not commit adultery, do you commit adultery? You who abhor idols, do you rob temples? You who boast in the law, do you dishonor God by breaking the law? As it is written: "God's name is blasphemed among the Gentiles because of you." Circumcision has value if you observe the law, but if you break the law, you have become as though you had not been circumcised. So then, if those who are not circumcised keep the law's requirements, will they not be regarded as though they were circumcised? The one who is not circumcised physically and yet obeys the law will condemn you who, even though you have the written code and circumcision, are a lawbreaker. A person is not a Jew who is one only outwardly, nor is circumcision merely outward and physical. No, a person is a Jew who is one inwardly; and circumcision is circumcision of the heart, by the Spirit, not by the written code. Such a person's praise is not from other people, but from God (Rom 2:17–29).

We have seen Paul address the world, meaning those outside of the church. In the previous section, Paul addressed the Gentile Christians in the church. In this section, Paul addressed the Jewish Christians in the church. Paul began this section by pointing out the benefits that they boasted. Paul never did say they should not boast in them, but he built on that very point to address their actions. The Jews had their name they could boast in, taking pride in being a *Jew,* one of God's chosen. They were able to boast in the law. Paul spoke of this advantage in the next chapter. They could boast in the fact that they were instructed to be guides to the blind and instructors to the foolish. Finally, they were able to boast in circumcision. All of these things spoke of identity and relationship; they were God's special people.

However, Paul continued to explain that although they did have much to boast in, they neglected key virtues—lifestyle and transformed hearts. They boasted in the law they were given, yet they broke the law continually. Their rationale was that they had special privileges since they were Jews. Others justified themselves because they were not as bad as the wicked pagans, or even the Gentiles for that matter. Paul spoke against this lifestyle saying they had become a reproach, and that the name of the Lord was blasphemed among the Gentles. What a demoralizing statement to be made. When Paul spoke of the Gentiles, he was speaking of the non-Jewish Christians in the church, their fellow church members. Paul just told the Jews, the ones that were self-righteous, that when the Gentiles saw their lifestyle, they were discouraged and even began to disparage the ways of the Lord. This was a wake-up call.

Paul brought everything to a finalizing point when

provoking them to think of the value of what they had. What was more important than having the law, being a Jew, and being circumcised? At first thought, the Jews would have thought that nothing was. For those were the three most important things about being a Jew. However, at the same time, Paul addressed their lifestyle to show them that there was an obvious problem.

This is what Paul wanted the Jews to learn: The one thing that was better than having the law was to have the law written upon one's heart; the one thing better than being a Jew outwardly was to be a Jew inwardly; the only thing better than outward circumcision was to have one's heart circumcised. Paul was continuing the message of Christ—he was trying to make it an issue of the heart.

The key problem Paul was addressing with the Jews was their attitudes that were judgmental and self-righteous. Furthermore, they were not even living upright themselves. The Jews were cascading into a reliance on their heritage and the law rather than on the mercy and grace of God through Jesus Christ. Lastly, they were ignoring their sins as they were more focused on judging others.

Paul was continuing to build his case he began in 1:18. The point he was attempting to make was that everyone was under sin. Paul began by addressing the world, then he addressed the Gentiles in the church, and in this recent portion, he addressed the Jews. The picture is becoming clearer; Paul was wanting them to know that he really was trying to address everyone, and he wanted everyone to know that they all were sinners. Paul continued to explain this in the following pages when he said that *all have sinned and fallen short of the glory of God*. We will see that this was all for a purpose; Paul wanted to present Christ as the one who justifies. People will only run to a savior when they realize they have sin in their hearts. People will only realize they are sinners when they are placed under a law to which they stand accountable. And when people realize they are sinners, they will realize the need for a savior.

Chapter Three

Paul is going to build a case to present Christ. Paul spent the last half of chapter one looking at the sin of the world. He wanted to clearly show that even those without the law have a responsibility because of the evident proof given through creation. The bottom line was that they would have to stand before God, and one day give account for their actions. But the message did not end there; the purpose of revealing their sin was to ready them for a savior.

In chapter two, Paul addressed the church in Rome, both the Gentiles and the Jews. Throughout the chapter, he clarified that they were all under a law that made them accountable before God for their actions. Paul's purpose was to reveal to everyone that there was no one without sin; therefore, there was no one without a need for a savior. Furthermore, Paul wanted to place everyone under the same standard. He wanted them to know that they *all* were sinners; and, therefore they *all* were in need of a savior. Finally, as Paul was writing to a diverse church of both Jews and Gentiles, he wanted to clarify that in Christ there was no difference between them.

In chapter three, Paul is going to build to the climax of the case he began to build in 1:18. He continued to build his case by asking three rhetorical questions. We will look at each question and the answer Paul gave in the comments below. After the case was built, Paul then turned the page and presented the answer to the problem of sin in every heart—Jesus Christ.

> What advantage, then, is there in being a Jew, or what value is there in circumcision? Much in every way! First of all, the Jews have been entrusted with the very words of God (Rom 3:1–2).

The Jews had long thought that they were special and that there was an advantage to being a Jew. However, hearing what Paul said about the pagans, Gentiles, and Jews all being under the same bondage of sin, they would have not felt like there was any advantage, or some might have been ready to contend with Paul that there was. Paul, understanding that this would raise some questions, clarified that there was an advantage; the Jews had been entrusted with the words of God. When we were walking through chapter two, we would have noticed that it was the Jews who had the law, not the Gentiles; the Gentiles were under the law of conscience. Paul would later explain in chapter seven that the purpose of the law was to reveal *right* and *wrong*. In Paul's thinking, it was quite an advantage to know such truth. Having the knowledge of right and wrong would impact their lives greatly. It did not save them from sin, but it would be a guide. The word of God was a light to the world.

The advantage of being Jews was that they had that light to follow.

> What if some were unfaithful? Will their unfaithfulness nullify God's faithfulness? Not at all! Let God be true, and every human being a liar. As it is written: "So that you may be proved right when you speak and prevail when you judge." (Rom 3:3–4).

This is a very good question. The reason Paul asked this rhetorical question was that there was a good likelihood that many Jews had this thought. Paul had revealed their sin to the point that some might have noticed themselves as lawbreakers, perhaps even covenant breakers. This generated the obvious question, "will our unfaithfulness nullify God's faithfulness?" It was a fair question. As Paul was introducing a salvation that included the Gentiles, the Jew would have thought it was perhaps a *new* contract. They were certain that the original contract made with Abraham was only for the Jews. Did God end the contract with the Jews and begin a new contract with the Gentiles? Since the Jews were unfaithful, did God retract His faithfulness from the contract? Paul's answer was concise: "Not at all." Paul continued to explain that people are capable of lying and being unfaithful, but God remains true. To say that God was unfaithful would make Him as unjust as humanity. Paul was keeping it simple; God had remained faithful. He kept his words few for now; in chapter eleven, Paul will explain in detail how the covenant with the Jews never ended. God wanted to ingraft the Gentiles into the covenant as well.

But if our unrighteousness brings out God's righteousness
more clearly, what shall we say? That God is unjust in
bringing His wrath on us? (I am using a human argument.) Certainly not! If that were so, how could God
judge the world? Someone might argue, "If my falsehood
enhances God's truthfulness and so increases His glory,
why am I still condemned as a sinner?" Why not say—as
some slanderously claim that we say—"Let us do evil that
good may result"? Their condemnation is just! (Rom
3:5–8)

Our Sin → Forgiveness → God's Glory

Paul brought another very relevant question to mind that
was surely in the minds of many of the Jews. If our unrighteousness brings about God's righteousness and His glory is
wrought in and through us, how can we be judged for that?
Would that not make God unjust? Here is the breakdown of
what is really happening. The first element is our sin. Next,
God brings forgiveness. Because of His merciful forgiveness,
God is then glorified. The question is then slanted to say,
"how can I be judged for God being glorified?" Paul's answer
was short and to the point for now; he will address this question in greater detail in chapter six. But at this time, his
answer was "certainly not!" He continued to explain that
people who think like this are *slanderous*. The very thought
of doing evil in order that good will result was worthy of
judgment in the mind of Paul. In hopes to justify themselves,
some were challenging the justice of God. Paul will carefully
address that issue, but not here. As we get to chapter six,
Paul will go into more detail on the matter in which we will
learn without a doubt that God is just. In fact, Paul

explained that God is the *only* one who is just. Furthermore, we will learn that it is because of Him who is just that we are all justified.

These rhetorical questions were intentionally placed by Paul. Firstly, they concluded his thoughts as he was building his case. Secondly, he placed them as an interlude in the case to deal with some questions that he was certain the Jews would have been thinking. Rather than let them struggle with the questions, he tackled them to help them understand. Lastly, these questions were used as a preface to where Paul was wanting to go. Each question was answered only briefly; each of these questions is a topic that Paul will go into further detail later in the letter. As for now, the next few verses are the finale of the case that Paul began to build in 1:18. He will bring the church to one conclusion—There is none righteous. We are all sinners. We all need a savior.

What shall we conclude then? Do we have any advantage? Not at all! For we have already made the charge that Jews and Gentiles alike are all under the power of sin. As it is written: "There is no one righteous, not even one; there is no one who understands; there is no one who seeks God. All have turned away, they have together become worthless; there is no one who does good, not even one." Their throats are open graves; their tongues practice deceit." "The poison of vipers is on their lips." "Their mouths are full of cursing and bitterness." "Their feet are swift to shed blood; ruin and misery mark their ways, and the way of peace they do not know." "There is no fear of God before their eyes." Now we know that whatever the law says, it says to those who are under the law, so that every mouth may be silenced and the whole world held accountable to God. Therefore no one will be declared righteous in God's sight by the works of the law; rather, through the law we become conscious of our sin (Rom 3:9–20).

Paul began by returning to the topic of Jewish heritage. Although there was an advantage to having the words of God entrusted to you, when it came to sin, there was no advantage—everyone is under the same bondage of sin. We now come to the point that Paul had been driving toward from 1:18; he wanted everyone to know, especially the Jews and Gentiles in the church in Rome, that all are under the same power of sin. Furthermore, all are guilty of sin and are without excuse. Finally, *all* will be held accountable for their own actions. This would lead them to the resolve which was Paul's very point—they needed a savior.

Paul made use of a plethora of Old Testament passages to support his case that all are lost under sin. Remember, the Jews would have appreciated the use of Jewish Scriptures. It is important to know that some of the passages used cannot and should not be taken literally. That was not the intent of Paul. The point of these passages was to reveal that everyone is lost in sin. There are many times Paul made use of Old Testament verses, and most, if not all, must be interpreted with his motive in mind. Every word in the quote might not be useful for the author's motive—what was the *point* Paul was trying to make? A familiar and comical example is the phrase we use when it is raining hard, we say, "It is raining cats and dogs!" Taken literally, it makes no sense and would confuse a person trying to parse out what it looks like to literally be raining *cats* and *dogs*. But those who can respect the point made by the speaker, are left with an understanding of the situation. What was the point of Paul using these Old Testament passages? To reveal from the Jewish Scripture that all were lost in sin and none were righteous.

Paul brought their minds back to chapter two where he showed them that both Jews and Gentiles were under the law. However, in verse 20, Paul clarified that even if they were to fulfill the law with perfection, it would not make them righteous. We now learn what the purpose of the law was. And if you look back on the ancient days when the law was given, you find it to be true. *The law was intended to make a person aware of sin.*

There was no saving power in the law, whether it was the law of Moses or the law of one's conscience. The law was simply to reveal sin. Paul had his audience right where he wanted them. They now knew that they were all sinners. They all knew that they were under a law and would be accountable for their actions. They now knew that even if they were to perfect the law, it still would not merit right-eousness. Now they were ready to hear the good news, the gospel of Jesus Christ.

> But now apart from the law the righteousness of God has been made known, to which the Law and the Prophets testify. This righteousness is given through faith in Jesus Christ to all who believe. There is no difference between Jew and Gentile, for all have sinned and fall short of the glory of God, and all are justified freely by His grace through the redemption that came by Christ Jesus. God presented Christ as a sacrifice of atonement, through the shedding of His blood—to be received by faith. He did this to demonstrate His righteousness, because in His forbearance He had left the sins committed beforehand

unpunished—He did it to demonstrate His righteousness
at the present time, so as to be just and the one who justifies those who have faith in Jesus (Rom 3:21–26).

The case was made; Paul had driven the point home—
there was no one righteous. It was at this moment that Paul
turned their attention to a righteousness that was available.
But not a righteousness from the law, but rather a righteousness peculiar to anything a person could accomplish.
Paul brought to light a few important features concerning
this righteousness: firstly, it was apart from the works of the
law; secondly, it was a righteousness from God; thirdly, this
righteousness was made known by the prophets; fourthly, it
was given through faith; lastly, it was for all who believe—
and it was only found in Jesus Christ. It was at this very
point that the Jews and Gentiles in the church would have
understood the salvation of God in a way they did not previously know. The many fallacies each would have had were
slowly dissipating as Paul made them aware of the truth.

To further build on the need for salvation, Paul took just
a little more time to illuminate the *sin* problem. In verses 23
and 24, he reminded them that "all have sinned and fall
short of the glory of God." It was for that very reason that
righteousness was made available to *all*—in Christ, there was
no difference between Jew and Gentile. In these verses, I
want to point out the intentional repetition that Paul used to
enforce a point. Again, notice how Paul made it clear that *all*
have sinned. That is everybody; Jew, Gentile, and the rest of
the world. There was no one who ever rose above this accusation except for Christ. However, Paul used this very point
to lead to the great salvation of Christ which justifies *all*. To
say it more clearly, *all* have sinned, but through Christ, *all*

are justified. Paul continued to explain that they were justified by the grace of God, through the redemption of Christ, and not by their own righteousness.

One of the key issues that Paul had to address with several churches in the first century was the matter of righteousness. In the case of the Galatians, they were attempting to be made righteous by returning to the works of the law (Gal 5:4). I don't know if we could say the same was true about the church in Rome, but Paul did want to help them understand this topic before they were to fall into the same error as the churches in Galatia.

In verses 25 and 26, Paul again used repetition to make a point. This time he was emphasizing that the salvation offered was because of the righteousness of God—*His righteousness*. In verse 25, God presented Jesus to be the atoning sacrifice, this was to demonstrate *His righteousness*. It is evident that it was not our own. As we saw back in verse 23, the only thing we contributed to the plan of salvation was our sin. God brought the righteousness. Verse 25 continues to speak of how God allowed previous sins to go unpunished until salvation was made ready, and in verse 26, Paul continued to say that God did this to demonstrate *His righteousness*. At this moment, the point had been made very clearly; whether you are a Jew or a Gentile, your salvation was supplied to you by the *righteousness of God*.

Paul made good use of this same wordplay at the end of the section. He had just said that all men are saved only by the righteousness of God. At the end of the section, Paul eloquently wrote, "as to be just and the one who justifies." The words *just* and *justify* are both rooted in the same Greek word righteousness. What Paul was saying is that we are saved by the righteousness of God. For He is the only one who is righteous/just. And out of His mercy, He placed *His* righteousness upon us, therefore making us righteous/just. He truly is the just one who makes just.

> Where, then, is boasting? It is excluded. Because of what law? The law that requires works? No, because of the law that requires faith. For we maintain that a person is justified by faith apart from the works of the law. Or is God the God of Jews only? Is He not the God of Gentiles too? Yes, of Gentiles too, since there is only one God, who will justify the circumcised by faith and the uncircumcised through that same faith. Do we, then, nullify the law by this faith? Not at all! Rather, we uphold the law (Rom 3:27–31).

Paul finished the section with a series of questions. All-in-all, the questions can be summed up in one simple question: "Where then is boasting?" This really is the most logical conclusion to everything we had just read concerning the salvation provided to us by Christ. We truly have no room to boast, and that was exactly the point that Paul was wanting to make here. So by way of wrapping up his thoughts, he summarized everything he had already said while adding that there is no room for boasting: there is no room for boasting because we are not justified by the law or any such works; there is no room for boasting because a person is justified only through Jesus Christ; there is no room to boast because God is God over the Jews and Gentiles alike; lastly, there is no room to boast because God will justify anyone regardless of circumcision and works. Paul was careful to place all the glory upon God and the work that was done through Christ. The reader would have understood clearly that there was truly no room to boast in what was so graciously given by God.

However, this being said, it did not leave the law nullified. This chapter marks one of the greatest transitions of all time. Paul took the Romans on a literary journey starting with them being lost in sin and their works of law to resting in the saving grace of a savior. This was truly a lot to take in. There was a grave need to explain a few more details. One of the biggest questions anyone might suggest is, does the grace of God and salvation by faith negate the law? Paul ended this chapter with a simple statement only to ready the reader for where he would go next. In chapter four, Paul is going to bring in Old Testament authority to prove that justification had always come by faith. However, we will continue to see as we already have that there was value in the law. Christ did not come to abolish the law but to fulfill it.

Chapter Four

Paul finished chapter three speaking of a righteousness that did not come from the works of the law, but by the grace and mercy of God. He clarified that it was for that reason that they had no room to boast. However, this was not to say that the law was put aside. Paul ended chapter three by saying that we do not nullify the law; rather, we uphold it. How do we reconcile the law and faith? Paul is going to bring Abraham into the argument to help clarify this matter.

> What then shall we say that Abraham, our forefather according to the flesh, discovered in this matter? If, in fact, Abraham was justified by works, he had something to boast about—but not before God. What does Scripture say? "Abraham believed God, and it was credited to him as righteousness." (Rom 4:1–3)

Paul was making an argument for righteousness by faith in the New Covenant, why then would he want to bring

Abraham into the picture? I think there are three credible reasons for Paul's decision: firstly, Abraham was the universally accepted father to all—both to the Gentiles and the Jews, but more so for the Jews. The Jews took pride in the fact that Abraham was their forefather (Matt 3:9; Luke 3:8; John 8:39). If Paul was going to convince the Jews, it would have to be through Abraham. Secondly, Abraham was truly the *poster child* for Christian faith. He is mentioned in the book of Hebrews along with many others, but I think we overlook the many times Abraham was asked to take a step in faith. It started when God asked him to leave Ur and go into a country he did not know. Then Abraham let Lot pick the land of his choice. Then God made a promise to Abraham that seemed to be impossible, so impossible that Abraham thought he had to intercede. After finally having a child, Abraham's faith was tested as he was asked to put Isaac on the altar. Abraham understood what it was like to take a step into the unknown. Lastly, Paul wanted to use Abraham in his argument because Abraham evidently struggled as anyone has. Yet, in his struggles, we read about Abraham living a life taking steps of faith in God. So when you want to use an Old Testament figure who was both authoritative *and* understood faith, Abraham was the best choice.

In these first few verses, Paul said that Abraham was not justified by works, meaning the law. That would have been problematic for most Jews. Abraham was righteous, no one would dare contend that truth—but how did he become righteous? The Jews argued that in order to become righteous, one had to uphold the law, and you, therefore, became righteous—justified by the law. However, Paul told them that Abraham was not justified in such a way. In fact, the law of Moses was not even in existence at the time of Abraham.

Paul quoted Genesis 15:6 saying, "Abraham believed God, and it was credited to him as righteousness." It was time for the Jews to rethink their theology. Somewhere down the line, the law became required to become righteous. But they were reminded in this chapter that was not how it was at the beginning; God credits his righteousness through faith.

> Now to the one who works, wages are not credited as a gift but as an obligation. However, to the one who does not work but trusts God who justifies the ungodly, their faith is credited as righteousness. David says the same thing when he speaks of the blessedness of the one to whom God credits righteousness apart from works: "Blessed are those whose transgressions are forgiven, whose sins are covered. Blessed is the one whose sin the Lord will never count against them." (Rom 4:4–8)

Paul introduced a logical argument to consider; if a person worked for his or her wages, they could not be considered a gift. Rather, they would be earned. His argument was posed against those who thought they were made righteous by doing the law. If they were made righteous by what they did, then their righteousness would be earned; it would no longer be a gift of grace by God through His mercy. If a person was able to earn righteousness, God would be *obligated* to give it, hence it would be no gift at all. Furthermore, if a person was able to earn his or her own righteousness, there would be no need for Jesus. Paul disagreed strongly with this ideology and clarified in chapter six that a person can only earn one thing on his own; through our sin, we earn only death. Our life comes as a gift from God. Paul continued to emphasize that righteousness is a gift and is credited. He was careful to take this approach to counter the already existing thoughts that some have earned their righteousness.

Paul brought David into his argument, which was a brilliant move. Paul had already gotten their attention with the use of Abraham, but to make use of David would strengthen his case all the more. Paul pointed out that David said the same thing about righteousness; it is not earned, but it is credited.

The word *credit* is as we would expect when using checkbook ledgers; one can add money to the account, and you would call that a credit. We are going to notice another play on words as Paul wanted to drive another important point. The word credit is used in this chapter about eleven times. The key is to know that God wants to credit our account with His righteousness, and David calls that a blessed thing. When God adds to our account, we are blessed. It is nothing we earn; it is freely given. However, in verse 8, David said "Blessed is the one whose sin the Lord *will never count against them*." The word used for *never count against* is the same as credit, but in the negative. Paul was trying to show them that it is a blessed thing when God *credits* righteousness to our account, and also when he chooses *not to credit* against our accounts for our sin—this is because of His forgiveness.

There is one theme that should be clear at this point: no one can *earn* righteousness from God. Paul continued to use the word *credit* for a reason; this is something given by God. And as we will see in the next section, it was given not by works of the law, but by faith. Paul was removing any presupposition that righteousness can be earned—it is and always has been a gift and a blessing from God.

Is this blessedness only for the circumcised, or also for the uncircumcised? We have been saying that Abraham's faith was credited to him as righteousness. Under what circumstances was it credited? Was it after he was circumcised, or before? It was not after, but before! And he received circumcision as a sign, a seal of the righteousness that he had by faith while he was still uncircumcised. So then, he is the father of all who believe but have not been circumcised, in order that righteousness might be credited to them. And he is then also the father of the circumcised who not only are circumcised but who also follow in the footsteps of the faith that our father Abraham had before he was circumcised. It was not through the law that Abraham and his offspring received the promise that he would be heir of the world, but through the righteousness that comes by faith. For if those who depend on the law are heirs, faith means nothing and the promise is worthless, because the law brings wrath. And where there is no law there is no transgression. Therefore, the promise comes by faith, so that it may be by grace and may be guaranteed to all Abraham's offspring—not only to those who are of the law but also to those who have the faith of Abraham. He is the father of us all. As it is written: "I have made you a father of many nations." He is our father in the sight of God, in whom he believed—the God who gives life to the dead and calls into being things that were not (Rom 4:9–17).

Paul was continuing his thought that God credits righteousness to a person apart from the works of the law, including circumcision. Paul just finished writing about the blessedness of having one's sins forgiven and being counted righteous. He followed up with the question in verse nine asking, "Is this blessedness only for the circumcised, or also for the uncircumcised?" He answered the question by reflecting upon the righteousness of Abraham. The law of Moses would not have come into existence for about another 600 years after Abraham. Paul's point was proven quite clearly; Abraham was righteous *before* the law and *before* circumcision (Gen 17). The question Paul was really wanting the Jews to consider is, *why would you then, as children of Abraham, require people to follow the law of Moses and be circumcised to become righteous when that is not how Abraham was made righteous?*

Through this passage, we learn that Abraham was credited righteousness because of his faith. The Old Testament passage says, "Abram believed the Lord, and He credited it to him as righteousness" (Gen 15:6). With this, it is important to make a couple of points. Abraham had faith, but it was not for his faith alone by which God credited righteousness. Action was required, or one might say *a demonstration* of one's faith. When James wrote his letter to the Christians, he told them that their faith was dead if it was not accompanied by actions. To qualify his argument, James also referenced Abraham saying this:

You foolish person, do you want evidence that faith without deeds is useless? Was not our father Abraham considered righteous for what he did when he offered his son Isaac on the altar? You see that his faith and his actions were working together, and his faith was made complete by what he did. And the scripture was fulfilled that says, "Abraham believed God, and it was credited to him as righteousness," and he was called God's friend.

You see that a person is considered righteous by what they do and not by faith alone (Jas 2:20–24).

This passage makes it clear that faith alone does nothing; faith must be accompanied by action. We see this demonstration as we survey the life of Abraham. He took a step of faith as he left Ur, going into a country he did not know. He took a step of faith when he laid Isaac on the altar. It was not that Abraham *claimed* to have faith, he *demonstrated* his faith. To claim to have faith and yet not do as God asked him to, would be a clear indication of a lack of faith. But Abraham believed God. It was for the reason of his faith *and* the actions that followed that God credited to him righteousness.

Before we continue, I want to reflect on an important question that was in part discussed before in the comments about Romans 3:20; If righteousness was provided through faith *before* the law, why was the law given? The answer Paul gave 3:20 was that the law was given to make a person conscious of sin. Paul will return to this point in 7:7–13 saying that if it were not for the law, we would not know what sin was. When Paul wrote to the churches in Galatia, he called the law a *schoolmaster* or *guardrail.* Imagine driving down the road. There are usually guardrails along the road when there is a steep slope or water along the edge. The guardrail ensures that with a little responsibility on your part, you stay on the road. The law was given in the Old Testament to guide them along the road while they did their best to try to live according to the standards of God. However, the plan of God would not be complete until Christ. This will be seen in chapter ten.

Paul wrapped up this section by reminding them that their father Abraham was not made righteous by the works of the law and circumcision, and neither will they. Works never made anyone righteous. The law never made anyone holy. Circumcision never transformed a person's heart. Righteousness cannot be earned, rather it is a gift from God that He credits to anyone who responds in faith, an active faith. And yes, Paul was clear and intentional with what he wrote, the gift is for *all*.

> Against all hope, Abraham in hope believed and so became the father of many nations, just as it had been said to him, "So shall your offspring be." Without weakening in his faith, he faced the fact that his body was as good as dead—since he was about a hundred years old— and that Sarah's womb was also dead. Yet he did not waver through unbelief regarding the promise of God but was strengthened in his faith and gave glory to God, being fully persuaded that God had power to do what He had promised. This is why "it was credited to him as righteousness." The words "it was credited to him" were written not for him alone, but also for us, to whom God will credit righteousness—for us who believe in Him who raised Jesus our Lord from the dead. He was delivered over to death for our sins and was raised to life for our justification (Rom 4:18–25).

"Against all hope." To fully understand what Paul was saying here, we need to understand what *hope* is. It is an *expectation, something you can look forward to.* When Abraham was asked to leave Ur and go into a land he did not know, it was against all hope. When he let Lot choose the seemingly best land, it was against all hope. When Abraham laid Isaac on the altar, it was against all hope. In each of these situations, Abraham had his plan that he could see into, he had hope and vision. But God's plan was different. The steps Abraham was asked to take did not make sense to him. Abraham tried to look beyond and into the plan of God, but he couldn't see and was left not knowing what God was doing—against all hope. But Abraham, trusting God, going against all hope, and taking a step into the unknown, was becoming a man of faith.

Yet it says that "Abraham in hope believed." When asked to take a step into what you cannot see, this is going against all hope; the question is, will we trust and take a step anyway? Abraham believed in God to the point of taking a step into the unknown. His faith in God was all he needed to know. The faith of Abraham took the unknown and shaped it into something good; whether it was reality or not, Abraham trusted that God would make it good. Consider Hebrews 11:17–19:

> By faith Abraham, when God tested him, offered Isaac as a sacrifice. He who had embraced the promises was about to sacrifice his one and only son, even though God had said to him, "It is through Isaac that your offspring will be reckoned." Abraham reasoned that God could even raise the dead, and so in a manner of speaking he did receive Isaac back from death.

Abraham reasoned that God was doing *something* good, even though it was unknown to him. So Abraham began to imagine just what God might have been doing. Abraham's best guess was that God would simply raise Isaac from the dead. It wasn't exactly how it went down, but the point is that Abraham took a step trusting that God was doing something good.

Notice the faith of Abraham; it wasn't blind faith. But if you consider the life of Abraham and all the many times his faith was tried and tested, you realize that Abraham was ready for this enormous test. Abraham trusted God because he had learned to trust God over many years.

Even though Abraham was often unsure of the road ahead of him, he had learned that God was leading him in good places—that is faith. And it was because of this faith that Abraham was willing to obey God and do what God asked him to do. Because of that faith brewing in the heart of Abraham, God accredited to him righteousness. And this is the point that Paul was trying to relay to the church in Rome.

The chapter concludes with two verses that provide us with a perfect summation of what Paul had been saying. God credits righteousness to us, the one true God, the one who raised Jesus from the dead. Jesus was delivered up to be killed in order to become the atonement for our sins. He was raised to life for our justification. For the Jew, and really for any reading, this would have driven the stake in—our righteousness, our justification, it all comes from God. Moreover, it is provided through the sacrifice of Jesus. We are made righteous by God. It is a gift through Jesus Christ.

Chapter Five

Years ago, when I was a teenager, my family would go up to Sault Ste. Marie to go salmon fishing. My dad would take us out on Saint Mary's River to troll. When you are trolling in a river as vast as Saint Mary's, it is hard to stay going straight. However, my dad knew where he wanted us to go. To ensure our *trajectory*, my dad would tell me to focus on one thing ahead of us; sometimes the bridge, or some other stationary object. Every turn I made with the steering wheel was with that object in mind. It would take a long time to troll through those waters. Sometimes I would be holding that wheel for what felt like forever. But while keeping our heading, we would reach the end goal. I like to think that this is a good analogy to how the Bible is laid out. There are so many events, obstacles, and moving parts. But there is one stationary goal that everything was pointing toward. The trajectory of everything was always aimed toward God's salvation for humanity—Jesus.

Paul spent the first few chapters of this letter showing

the church that everyone was under the same power of sin and that they were not saved by the works of the law. Furthermore, Paul revealed that just as *all* were lost in sin, God desired to save *all* by His grace through justification found only in Christ. With this being said, we have to remember that Paul was writing to a church which were Christians—they were justified. However, as we learned in the introduction, their knowledge was based on very little teaching. Paul was wanting to show them what salvation looked like. He wanted them to understand grace, justification, and the truth about baptism. This is why chapter five begins with, "Therefore, since we have been justified..." Paul was writing to Christians. But to this point, he is going to build on that very thought; *what does it mean to be justified?* Furthermore, *what does it mean to have life and hope?* This is where Paul is going to direct their minds through this chapter. I like to call this chapter *the trajectory toward salvation.* You will see why on the pages below.

> Therefore, since we have been justified through faith, we have peace with God through our Lord Jesus Christ, through whom we have gained access by faith into this grace in which we now stand. And we boast in the hope of the glory of God. Not only so, but we also glory in our sufferings, because we know that suffering produces perseverance; perseverance, character; and character, hope. And hope does not put us to shame, because God's love has been poured out into our hearts through the Holy Spirit, who has been given to us (Rom 5:1–5).

The first verse of this chapter verifies that this letter was

intended for Christians. Paul was writing to the church in
Rome, and it is evident that although they were diverse and
had minimal knowledge of salvation, they were Christians,
nonetheless. However, this letter was and is quite useful for
the unsaved as well. As we will see in the next chapter, this
letter reveals the path of salvation. Whether you are a Christian or not, this letter has one purpose; to reveal the founda-
tional truths of salvation.

This chapter begins by saying, "Therefore, since we have
been justified through faith." We have been talking about
justification for a few chapters now, but what is justification?
It is as simple as *to render just or innocent*. We also get the
idea of justification when considering modern *Word*
programs; justification is to make straight that which was
crooked. The idea we are given by Paul is that we were once
crooked and guilty of our sin, but then, through Christ, we
were justified—we were made innocent. Christ took our sin
upon His shoulders. This is what Peter spoke about saying,
"'He himself bore our sins' in His body on the cross, so that
we might die to sins and live for righteousness; 'by His
wounds you have been healed'" (1 Pet 2:24). Through the
sacrifice of Christ, our sins were removed and the righteousness of Christ was placed upon us—we were justified.
But Paul wanted the church to know what it meant to be
justified.

Since we have been justified, *we have peace with God.*
What a gift! We learn from passages like Ephesians 2:12 and
Romans 5:10 that before people turn to Christ, they are
enemies with God. That is a terrifying reality if you consider
the unfolding drama of the Old Testament. The problem
was sin; sin has always been the problem. Isaiah 59:2 says
that it is sin that separates us from God. Therefore, it is

simple math to assume that if you remove the sin, you remove the reproach; that is exactly how it works. Before Christ, while people are living in their sin, they are enemies with God. But when they turn to Christ, He justifies them, rendering them innocent of their guilt as He takes that sin upon His shoulders through the work of the cross. Those people, now with their sins forgiven, can stand before God knowing that He looks at them with favor. That was why Paul spoke of access by faith *into grace*. Grace is the idea of receiving favor from God. Through Christ, we can stand assured that God looks at us in favor.

The passage speaks about boasting. Boasting is not always looked upon fondly, but there are a couple of things Paul said a Christian can boast about. One of these things we can boast in is the *hope of the glory of God*. We gave the definition of hope in the previous chapter; *an expectation or something to look forward to*. If you look at the way Paul worded this verse, I don't think he was necessarily talking about our future home and so on. I believe he was speaking of God being glorified in our lives as He is allowed to justify us and transform our lives. And we should be able to look forward to such glory; our lives being changed and God being glorified for the marvelous work of His hands. All in all, in Christ, we can boast.

The second thing Paul says we can boast in is our sufferings. I want to help where the English language might not be so helpful. In verse two, Paul spoke of *boasting in the hope of the glory of God*. In verse three, Paul said, "but we also glory in our sufferings." The word Paul used for *glory* is the same Greek word for *boast* in the previous verse. We can and should boast in our sufferings. But the question is, why? Anyone who is left asking this very question is simply using common sense. How does it make any sense to boast in our sufferings? Of course, Paul anticipated that some would wonder this, so in the following verses, Paul gave the answer we are looking for.

We should boast in our suffering because suffering shapes us. *Suffering produces perseverance.* Perseverance is another word for patience. Many of us have often prayed for patience. At the same time, many of us pray that God would take our suffering away. But we need to be mindful that the suffering might be an answer to your prayer. But even if you didn't pray for it, God wants to see His children grow. *Perseverance [produces] character.* Character is the rating of a person. Even today, we judge others by their character; some have good character, and some have bad character. Our suffering is intended to develop patience, which in turn develops good character. *Character [produces] hope.* I know that in our suffering it is hard to see past the dark cloud, but if we see it through, in the end, we will have more to look forward to than we ever thought possible.

Hope is what everyone needs. Paul spoke of hope when writing to the church in Corinth. He said that if we only have hope for this life, we are a people most to be pitied (1 Cor 15:19). Through our suffering, God wants to develop in our hearts patience, character, and a hope that we have a God shaping our lives and a home prepared with Him in eternity—that is hope—that is something to look forward to. Paul concluded this section by saying that this hope does not make one ashamed. How could such a glorious thing be something to be ashamed about? People drive up in their fancy cars proud and ready to show it off. If people land a great job, they proudly share it with all their friends. A woman gets engaged and flashes her ring for all to see. There are things in life that are simply designed by their own right to be proud of. When we stand before the world with this hope that we have through Christ, it is nothing to be ashamed of. Quite the contrary, Paul said we should boast.

> You see, at just the right time, when we were still power-less, Christ died for the ungodly. Very rarely will anyone die for a righteous person, though for a good person someone might possibly dare to die. But God demon-strates His own love for us in this: While we were still sinners, Christ died for us. Since we have now been justi-fied by His blood, how much more shall we be saved from God's wrath through Him! For if, while we were God's enemies, we were reconciled to Him through the death of His Son, how much more, having been reconciled, shall we be saved through His life! Not only is this so, but we also boast in God through our Lord Jesus Christ, through whom we have now received reconciliation (Rom 5:6–11).

At what moment is a person saved? This is a good ques-tion for today as it was in the first century. If we were to ask a Jew during those early days, they would say a person was saved when he or she was able to accomplish the law. In essence, they would have to be good in order to be justified. That is not what Paul wrote here. It is when people are powerless and lost in sin, that is when God is able to trans-form them. People do not need to change first, they simply need to turn to Him in faith saying, "Lord..."

Christ was put on the cross at just the right time. The Jews thought they were in charge of the devious plan when they plotted to crucify Jesus, but it was God's plan. Peter announced this truth in his sermon on the Day of Pentecost, saying, "This man [Jesus] was handed over to you by God's deliberate plan and foreknowledge; and you, with the help of wicked men, put Him to death by nailing Him to the cross" (Acts 2:23). Peter also suggested that the plan of salvation through Christ was set in motion before the foundation of the world (1 Pet 1:19–20). One might ask why Jesus did not come sooner. There was so much sin manifested in the four-thousand years prior to Christ. We don't know the answer to that. What we do know is that Jesus was sent deliberately by God, fulfilling a perfect plan of salvation, *at just the right time.*

How *good* does a person have to be to demonstrate love for another person in such a selfless way as Christ did? But not just *another* person, a *sinful* person. Paul said that a person will rarely die for even a *righteousness* person. And perhaps it just might be possible that one would die for a *good* person. But not for a sinner. This was the point. Paul wanted the church in Rome to know just how great a sacrifice Jesus was. They didn't become good enough to earn anything. The law did not give them any merit. It was not when they became righteous that Jesus died. But while they were living in sin, that is when Jesus willingly went to the cross. This *goodness* of God and Jesus was spoken of back in Romans 2:4. The Romans were learning a valuable truth; salvation was not because of *their* goodness, but the kindness and goodness of God.

Since they were justified, there are wonderful benefits that Paul wanted to make them aware of. First Paul said that they were saved from the wrath of God. The Jews especially were well acquainted with the stories of the Old Testament. Therein were plenty of examples of the wrath of God. The assurance that one could be saved from that wrath was a marvelous gift. Paul explained that they were reconciled to God through the death of Jesus. Furthermore, upon being reconciled, they had life. It is quite simple how this works. As I mentioned before, there has only been one thing that has ever separated humanity from God—sin (Isa 59:2). That sin made us enemies with God. Jesus took that sin from us as he went to the cross. We are therefore reunited with God—reconciliation. While we are in Christ, we no longer have to fear the wrath of God; rather, we enjoy being truly alive. This is salvation.

> Therefore, just as sin entered the world through one man, and death through sin, and in this way death came to all people, because all sinned—To be sure, sin was in the world before the law was given, but sin is not charged against anyone's account where there is no law. Nevertheless, death reigned from the time of Adam to the time of Moses, even over those who did not sin by breaking a command, as did Adam, who is a pattern of the one to come. But the gift is not like the trespass. For if the many died by the trespass of the one man, how much more did God's grace and the gift that came by the grace of the one man, Jesus Christ, overflow to the many! Nor can the gift of God be compared with the result of one man's sin: The judgment followed one sin and brought condemnation, but the gift followed many trespasses and brought justification. For if, by the trespass of the one man, death reigned through that one man, how much more will those who receive God's abundant provision of grace and of the gift of righteousness reign in life through the one man, Jesus Christ! Consequently, just as one trespass resulted

in condemnation for all people, so also one righteous act
resulted in justification and life for all people. For just as
through the disobedience of the one man the many were
made sinners, so also through the obedience of the one
man the many will be made righteous (Rom 5:12–19).

Clear as black and white. That is what we say when a
matter is defined with clarity, and when a situation has lost
all of its gray matter. That is what Paul did in this passage.
Sin comes from the one man, Adam. Justification comes from
the one man, Jesus. Done. That is as black and white as one
can paint it. That really is as simple as this passage is, but I
will take time to explain a few more things.

While revealing the origin of sin, Paul returned their
attention to 3:23 reminding them that all have sinned. It is
true that sin entered through only one man. But the fact is,
all people sinned after Adam as well. Consequently, death
came to everyone.

What is curious is that Paul said that sin was in the
world from the time of Adam. In a previous chapter, Paul
said that God had left the sins committed beforehand
unpunished (3:25). He went on to say that God did that to
demonstrate His righteousness. When Paul wrote to the
church in Corinth, he said the power of sin was the law (1
Cor 15:56). As Paul explained here in Romans, the sins
committed before the law were left unpunished. Before the
law, sins were not charged against anyone's account. But
when the law came, the sting of death came. This raised a
question that Paul will address in chapter seven; does this
make the law evil? The answer is obviously "No!" The sting
and condemnation of the law were necessary. This will be
answered more clearly when we get to chapter seven.

The passage we are looking at is also designed to draw a contrast, as I want to reveal to you on the chart below:

The One Man—Adam

Trespass (sin) of one → Many died
Trespass of one → Judgment
Trespass of one → Condemnation
Disobedience of one → All are sinful

The One Man—Jesus

Gift provided by One → Provision of grace
Gift provided by One → Righteousness
Righteousness of One → Justification
Obedience of One → Many made righteous

The Two Men

The point Paul was wanting to make is that humanity is sinful and in need of a savior. But the emphasis is not on man's sin, but on the "how much more." This phrase is mentioned several times in this passage. Yes, a person was lost in the trespass, but there is something *better* available—the gift of God through Jesus Christ. This gift is not earned. It is given freely. It is not given because of our righteousness, but because of the righteousness of Christ. Salvation is through Jesus Christ.

The law serves as a purpose in the unfolding plan of God. This will lead into the next section as we talk about the *trajectory toward salvation.*

The law was brought in so that the trespass might
increase. But where sin increased, grace increased all the
more, so that, just as sin reigned in death, so also grace
might reign through righteousness to bring eternal life
through Jesus Christ our Lord (Rom 5:20–21).

God was setting humanity on a trajectory. It is easy to
look at the law as an isolated Old Testament concept, while
the New Testament is covered by the blood of Christ. And
many students of the Bible, because they do not know how to
reconcile the two, sever the testaments from one another. But
I believe it is more helpful to view the plan of salvation as a
linear set of events; each event is plotted on the timeline
before time began.

The timeline of events began before the foundation of
the earth (1 Pet 1:20). What I mean, and as Peter was clear
to state, is that the plan of salvation began before the world
began. God had set it in motion before the earth began to
rotate. Then as you progress along the plan, we come to the
days of Adam and all the way to Israel's time in Egypt.
Granted, this covers nearly 2,500 years. During this time,
they did not have the law; however, as we saw above, sin was
still present. Sin was present because they had creation and
the many works of God to reflect on (Rom 1:18–21).
Furthermore, they had the law of conscience that was
engrained to some degree in each person (Rom 2:12–16).
But out of His mercy and revealing His righteousness, God
left those sins unpunished.

Down the timeline, now during the time of Moses, God
brought the law in order to reveal His nature. It was His
special way to begin to create a people that could emulate
His character. The law would change everything. When

God gave Moses the law on Mount Sinai, although they were unaware of His intentions, God was drawing them closer to Himself. The law would not merely be rules, it would bring life to the sting of death (1 Cor 15:56). The law would demand a responsibility and accountability to one's own actions. But this was all for a divine purpose.

One does not have to read long in the Old Testament to see that the people continually struggled to uphold the law. But God knew they would never be able to live as upright as the law, for the law revealed the perfect nature of God. But for a person to uphold the law perfectly was never the point. The law was never intended to make a person holy (Heb 10). As we saw above, its purpose was to reveal sin. The law was not intended to reconcile a person back to God. It was designed to reveal God's character. But therein lies the problem. The character of God was revealed in the law, the law that, even on our best days and with all our effort, we will fail miserably at obeying. We simply do not have the capability to be just.

Therefore, if we view the plan of God as a linear timeline all planned by God ahead of time, we would notice a marvelous truth. The law was never intended to be the answer but had one purpose—to point us to Christ. This is why Jesus said He came to fulfill the law (Matt 5:17). Paul also speaks of Christ being the culmination of the law (Rom 10:4). If people sever the Old Testament from the New, they miss the greatest course of events playing out in all of time. From before the world began, and through all four thousand years of the Old Testament, God was leading the people to Christ.

When Paul asked about the law being brought in to cause sin to increase, it was to set them up to realize that they needed a savior. God always knew people would fall short under the law. His plan before time began was to have each person resting in the grace of Christ. That is why I call this chapter the *trajectory toward salvation*. The fact is, we have always been on a trajectory toward salvation—the marvelous plan of God through Jesus.

Chapter Six

The previous chapters have been taking us on a journey toward salvation. Paul was writing to Christians, so one might ask, why was Paul detailing for them salvation? They had limited knowledge of salvation, and Paul was wanting to strengthen their knowledge, and ultimately their walk. Paul first established that everyone was lost in sin. He added that no one can justify himself by the works of the law, nor was anyone good enough on his own. Paul finally presented the one who could justify them—Jesus Christ. Paul spent chapter four showing, through Abraham, that a person was justified not by works, but by an active faith. As Paul finished chapter five, he showed them that the law was brought in order that the trespass might increase. The purpose of that, as we discussed, was that the need for Christ would be greater, and God would richly pour out His grace on those who call on Jesus. Paul transitioned into His next thought with a rhetorical question; "What shall we say, then? Shall we go on sinning so that grace may increase?"

What shall we say, then? Shall we go on sinning so that
grace may increase? By no means! We are those who have
died to sin; how can we live in it any longer? Or don't you
know that all of us who were baptized into Christ Jesus
were baptized into His death? We were therefore buried
with Him through baptism into death in order that, just
as Christ was raised from the dead through the glory of
the Father, we too may live a new life (Rom 6:1–4).

It is a logical question, and without any preconceived
ideas of Christianity, it really does make sense. If our sin
causes God's grace to abound, is it really all that bad? Paul
briefly touched on this topic back in 3:5 when he asked
another rhetorical question; "But if our unrighteousness
brings out God's righteousness more clearly, what shall we
say? That God is unjust in bringing wrath on us?" He
approached it a little differently here, but the same idea is
present; should I or can I keep on sinning? Paul's answer was
the same as before; "By no means!" But now Paul will
explain why not.

The simple reason why we should not live in sin is if we
are Christians, we have died to sin, therefore how can we live
in it any longer? That really is the answer in its short form.
But as Paul often did, he went deeper. How did we die to
sin? We died to sin when we were baptized into Christ. Paul
expounded by giving us an analogy to parallel our baptism
experience—the death, burial, and resurrection of Christ.
We started off living a life of sin, apart from God. But when
we chose to become a Christian, we took the step in faith to
be baptized, dying to our sin. Just as Christ died, we died to
sin. Christ was buried, in the same way, we buried our old
nature. And as Jesus was raised to a new life, a person who is

baptized is raised up as a new person in Christ. This is salvation.

> For if we have been united with Him in a death like His, we will certainly also be united with Him in a resurrection like His. For we know that our old self was crucified with Him so that the body ruled by sin might be done away with, that we should no longer be slaves to sin— because anyone who has died has been set free from sin (Rom 6:5–7).

Baptism plays a tremendous role in one's salvation. It is more than a mere act of obedience; it is an act of obedience that led to salvation. Many scholars rightfully note that water baptism, as we see it in the New Testament, was inseparable from salvation. And in this passage, Paul continued to explain the life people have after they have been baptized.

When people are baptized into Jesus Christ, they are united with Him in death. But that is not where it ends because Jesus did not stay in the grave. Just as people are united in a death like His, they are also united with Jesus's life after He was resurrected. It is this transition from the old body to the new body that freed us from the bondage of sin. The old nature was enslaved to sin. *That* sinful nature was put to death. When we came out of the water, the sinful nature stayed dead, the new arose alive in Christ, dead to sin. Christians are truly alive.

Coming back to Paul's rhetorical question, this is why we can't willfully live in sin. The purpose of this new life is that we are freed from sin. If we are free, we would not be walking in ways that harm us and displease God. Later in this chapter, Paul explains further that we are slaves to whom we obey. We will address that in its time. For now, the one thing we know is that as a baptized Christian, our sinful nature is dead and a new person rose up out of the water a new creation. Paul wrote to the church in Corinth about this matter saying, "Therefore, if anyone is in Christ, the new creation has come: The old has gone, the new is here! (2 Cor 5:17). A baptized Christian is a new creation.

> Now if we died with Christ, we believe that we will also live with Him. For we know that since Christ was raised from the dead, He cannot die again; death no longer has mastery over Him. The death He died, He died to sin once for all; but the life He lives, He lives to God (Rom 6:8–10).

"Now if we died to Christ." At the beginning of this chapter, Paul clarified how we died; we died to sin when we were baptized (6:3). Since we died with Christ in baptism, the expectation is that we live with him in our life. Notice the parallel Paul was continually trying to make with Christ and our baptism. Christ died and was raised to life—therefore sin has no mastery over Him. We died and were raised to life—sin and death no longer have mastery over us. Furthermore, this life we live, we are expected to live unto God.

We will see in the next few verses that, as a baptized Christian, sin does not have any power over us. However, we now have a choice. But that is the beauty of the victory brought by Christ—the free choice to choose to do right.

> In the same way, count yourselves dead to sin but alive to God in Christ Jesus. Therefore do not let sin reign in

your mortal body so that you obey its evil desires. Do not offer any part of yourself to sin as an instrument of wickedness, but rather offer yourselves to God as those who have been brought from death to life; and offer every part of yourself to Him as an instrument of righteousness. For sin shall no longer be your master, because you are not under the law, but under grace (Rom 6:11–14).

"In the same way..." In what way was Paul referring? He was launching from the previous verse where it says, "The death [Jesus] died, He died to sin once for all; but the life He lives, He lives to God." So, in what way? In the way that Christ died to sin and lived unto God. We are urged by Paul to do the same—count ourselves dead to sin and alive to God. It is a perfect parallel.

Because we are dead to sin and alive to Christ, we have an obligation to live like it. It is not that sin will no longer be an issue, but rather that we are not enslaved by sin any longer. We are free. Speaking to people who were free to choose, Paul told them not to let sin have any foothold. Furthermore, he urged them not to offer themselves to sin. I have always liked the King James version where it says not to "yield yourself..." Sin will always try to take hold, but it is our choice to yield to it or not. Paul spoke of this freedom and choice in his letter to the Galatians; he wrote, "You, my brothers and sisters, were called to be free. But do not use your freedom to indulge the flesh; rather, serve one another" (Gal 5:13).

Paul encouraged the church in Rome to *yield* themselves as an instrument to God. This is all possible through being dead to sin through baptism in Jesus Christ. The law had us in bondage, for all it could do was reveal our sin; it could not free us. But through the grace of God, we are made free.

> What then? Shall we sin because we are not under the law but under grace? By no means! Don't you know that when you offer yourselves to someone as obedient slaves, you are slaves of the one you obey—whether you are slaves to sin, which leads to death, or to obedience, which leads to righteousness? But thanks be to God that, though you used to be slaves to sin, you have come to obey from your heart the pattern of teaching that has now claimed your allegiance. You have been set free from sin and have become slaves to righteousness (Rom 6:15–18).

We have choices that must be made. We are set free by the blood of Christ, and therefore we have choices. People can choose to continue to walk in sin and remain enslaved by the very thing they were set free from. Or that same person can walk in obedience, leading to righteousness. One thing Paul wanted to make very clear in this passage was that every choice has a consequence. Living a sinful life means you have chosen to surrender yourself as a slave to sin once again. This choice will lead to death. When people choose to live in obedience, they make God their master. This choice leads to life.

Paul took a moment to praise the church in Rome in regard to what he had been saying. As everyone, the church in Rome used to live in sin and enslaved by its snare. But Paul said they learned to obey. They were set free from sin, but the most amazing part is that they *became* slaves to righteousness. Christ sets us free from sin through the work on the cross. A person can choose to be set free from sin, but it is another thing and a little more difficult to choose to become a slave to righteousness. But God has called us for this purpose and has given us everything we need to be free and to live for Him. The truth is that when we truly understand all that He has done for us, we will find it to be a worthy task to live for God.

> I am using an example from everyday life because of your human limitations. Just as you used to offer yourselves as slaves to impurity and to ever-increasing wickedness, so now offer yourselves as slaves to righteousness leading to holiness. When you were slaves to sin, you were free from the control of righteousness. What benefit did you reap at that time from the things you are now ashamed of? Those things result in death! But now that you have been set free from sin and have become slaves of God, the benefit you reap leads to holiness, and the result is eternal life. For the wages of sin is death, but the gift of God is eternal life in Christ Jesus our Lord (Rom 6:19–23).

Paul took them on the most practical path possible; he had them consider both paths—consider the benefits of sin compared to the benefits of obedience. Paul was very logical, and he liked to help people *think*. On many occasions, Paul went into the synagogue and *reasoned* with the people (Acts 17:2). When writing this letter to the church in Rome, Paul could have just told them how it was, but he wanted them to understand the reasoning. It will always go further when you help someone understand, rather than simply expect blind obedience.

The first thing Paul had them consider was the benefits they reaped from living in their past sin. He first points out how that style of living left them with shame. But further-more, as they reasoned among themselves the benefits of sin, they would have found that there are no benefits. In the moment, sin seems great. But there is no sin with a lasting reward, in this life, or eternally. If a person were to consider the benefits of adultery, murder, coveting, lying, lust, and all the like, all you have are shameful and regretful repercus-sions. This was what Paul wanted them to see. When consid-ering the life of sin, it's not just that God doesn't want you to have it. The truth is, you really don't want it either. Some-times we think we do, but when we *think* and consider the benefits of sin, we will realize the same thing the church in Rome did—there is no good that could come from sin.

Sin does not only have immediate repercussions on this earth; sin leads to death. This death is not necessarily a phys-ical death, but a separation between us and God. The fleeting pleasures of sin are not worth sacrificing eternity. The benefit of the wages of sin is death. It simply is not worth it. There you have it—sin exposed. Now the choice is yours.

Paul then had them consider the benefits of obedience. What is the benefit of living a life of faithfulness, truth, doing right, etc.? Paul said it leads to holiness. What is the benefit of holiness? Holiness leads to eternal life. The reward far outweighs the cost. This is why eternal life is called a *gift*. Because even after we live a life of obedience, we still come far from earning it. Yet like sin, obedience does not only have eternal repercussions; it directly impacts life on earth. It becomes quickly evident that living a life of faithfulness, truth, doing right, and all the other elements of obedience, simply reaps a better life. Consider *faithfulness* in a marriage —you just might make it to the end. Consider the effect of *truthfulness* in the workplace—job promotions and good standing with your employer will be yours. The benefit of obedience is not just to get to heaven, it is to have a good life while we are here. The benefits are all in our favor, and all we are asked to do is live an obedient and upright life. Once we *reason* as Paul asked, we will notice that it is well worth it. An obedient life is a good life.

Romans chapter six can be summed up in a simple phrase, "Don't you get it? As a baptized Christian, you are free. You now have the ability to choose your master. You can choose sin or obedience. Be warned and be aware; there are consequences for every decision you make."

Paul loved the church in Rome. And as Christians, he wanted them to be well aware of the life that is becoming of Christians and the benefits of walking upright. Paul wanted them to understand that a life in Christ did not only mean forgiveness but also a newness of character. With every stroke of the pen, Paul was giving the church instruction on how to walk in this new life in Christ.

Chapter Seven

A contract is an agreement between two or more parties. Contracts come in all shapes and sizes, but have one thing in common; they have the duties each party is to perform within the contractual bond. In some contracts, there are consequences for breaking the contract. What most contracts have are also the ways, if any, one of the parties can break free from the contract and duties therein. Contracts are not new to any civilization or ethnic group. This is why Paul was wise to make use of this item of common knowledge to explain his point.

Paul had made a great effort to lay out before us the path of salvation. He took us from understanding that we are all sinners to being ones surrendered to a justified life in Christ through water baptism. However, the intent of Paul to this point had been to reveal a justification that is in Christ and apart from the law. In chapter six, Paul used the symbol of baptism to illustrate how we die to sin; our sinful nature is buried and we are raised to a new life in Christ. In chapter seven, Paul is going to connect our baptismal death to freedom from the law. Yet, while we are dead to the law, Paul will also make it clear that the law does have value, but it holds no power to save. We are going to separate chapter seven into three easy sections that should help us to understand better what Paul was trying to say to the church in Rome.

> Do you not know, brothers and sisters—for I am speaking to those who know the law—that the law has authority over someone only as long as that person lives? For example, by law a married woman is bound to her husband as long as he is alive, but if her husband dies, she is released from the law that binds her to him. So then, if she has sexual relations with another man while her husband is still alive, she is called an adulteress. But if her husband dies, she is released from that law and is not an adulteress if she marries another man. So, my brothers and sisters, you also died to the law through the body of Christ, that you might belong to another, to Him who was raised from the dead, in order that we might bear fruit for God. For when we were in the realm of the flesh, the sinful passions aroused by the law were at work in us, so that we bore fruit for death. But now, by dying to what once bound us, we have been released from the law so that we serve in the new way of the Spirit, and not in the old way of the written code (Rom 7:1–6).

Paul introduced an illustration to help them understand that they were not under the law anymore. He brought their attention to a marriage contract. The point he was making with the contract is that it becomes void upon the death of either party involved. With this, Paul made the claim that the contract that once bound them to the law was void. But the question we have to ask now is, what or who died to annul the contract?

Some have suggested that it was the law that died. The idea painted with this ideology is that the law is dead, and we are no longer under it (married to it). We are therefore free to remarry (be united with Christ). At a quick glance, this view seems very plausible, but as we read further, we quickly learn that this is not what Paul had in mind. It is suggested by many that Paul was likely accused of *antinomianism* (anti-law). Yet, Paul was very clear in his writings to prove that the law was *not* annulled (Rom 3:31). And in the next section, Paul is going to speak of the value of the law. The contract was ended due to a death, but it was not the law that died.

Some have suggested that it was the death of Christ that ended the contract. This idea suggests that Christ died in order for the new covenant to begin. Even in Hebrews 9:16, we read that the Testator must die before the New Testament would begin. We also know that it is only through the death of Christ that we are set free. While all this is true, I do not think this is what Paul had in mind either, nor does it fit well in the contract illustration given by Paul. For a marriage contract to end, it must be the death of one of the partners *in* the contract to nullify the contract between the two. The contract we are speaking of is a bond between *us* and the *law*. There was a death to end the contract, but it clearly was not the death of Christ.

If it was not the death of Christ, nor the death of the law that ended the contract, we are only left with one other member enslaved by that contractual bond—us, our death. You might ask, *when did I die?* As a Christian, you died in baptism. This is the point that Paul made in chapter six. We died and were made alive in Christ. We live a new life, and that inherently means that we are free from the former slavery of sin *and* the contractual bond of the law. Paul clarified this point in 7:4 when he stated, "...you also died to the law...." I believe the picture Paul was trying to make was that before we came to Christ, we were *married* to the law, in certain words. The only way to break a marriage contract was death. Christ did not come to abolish the law. Paul had no intention to nullify the law. Between us and the law, it was not the law that had to die—it was us. Our baptismal death ended the contract with the law, allowing us to be united with another as Paul also says in 7:4, "that you might belong to another, to Him who was raised from the dead."

It is important to be mindful of the intent of Paul when he used this illustration; he was helping the church in Rome to understand how the law plays into salvation. Paul wanted them to know the power and impact of their baptism, but also that this new life in Christ was not because of their righteousness through the law. But at this point, the logical question of any Jew would be, *what then is the purpose of the law?* In the next two sections, Paul is going to answer this.

What shall we say, then? Is the law sinful? Certainly not! Nevertheless, I would not have known what sin was had it not been for the law. For I would not have known what coveting really was if the law had not said, "You shall not covet." But sin, seizing the opportunity afforded by the commandment, produced in me every kind of coveting. For apart from the law, sin was dead. Once I was alive apart from the law; but when the commandment came, sin sprang to life and I died. I found that the very commandment that was intended to bring life actually brought death. For sin, seizing the opportunity afforded by the commandment, deceived me, and through the commandment put me to death. So then, the law is holy, and the commandment is holy, righteous and good. Did that which is good, then, become death to me? By no means! Nevertheless, in order that sin might be recognized as sin, it used what is good to bring about my death, so that through the commandment sin might become utterly sinful (Rom 7:7–13).

I recently heard someone talk about the law and their frustration with other religious groups that adhere to it as the Jews did. Out of their frustration, this person spoke of just throwing the law out the window in lieu of grace. After all, we are not under the law anymore. So, in his defense, why couldn't we just throw the law out? After reading the first six chapters of Romans, one might be a bit perplexed as to what Paul really thinks about the law. Furthermore, it is suspected that some believed that Paul was a supporter of antinomianism. Did Paul *throw the law out the window?* In this passage, Paul is going to make a few points that will help us to see how he views the law as a New Testament Christian.

It is a valid question up to this point; *is the law sinful?* The answer is, *certainly not.* But why not? Paul's answer was simple; he would not have known what sin was if it were not for the law. And as we saw in Romans 3:20, the very intent of the law was to reveal sin. But as we have seen, the law had no power to take away sin, nor was anyone deemed righteous by doing the law.

Paul made a great point in verse 13 when he asked, "Did that which is good, then, become the death of me?" He called the law good to agree with the previous verse where he calls the law holy, righteous, and good. But did the law, which is so good, bring about our death? The answer again is no, but it is important to understand what Paul was trying to help us understand. He was bringing our minds back to the same thing he said back in Romans 5:20, "The law was brought in so that the trespass might increase." But why would we want the trespass to increase? This is what we see here in 7:13. Why would I want my sin to become *utterly sinful?* As I pointed out in the comments on 5:20, there is one reason: to prepare us for the saving grace of Jesus.

God wanted to pour His grace upon them, but if they saw no need for such grace, why would they accept it? However, through the law, people's sins are revealed. They realized—I realized that I am a sinner, and a pretty bad one at that. All the law does is reveal, reveal, and reveal. That is all the law does; it smacks me in the face reminding me how sinful I am. But because I know I am a sinner, I know that I need the forgiveness of Jesus, the saving power of a savior. So yes, the law is good; it points me toward Christ.

> We know that the law is spiritual; but I am unspiritual, sold as a slave to sin. I do not understand what I do. For what I want to do I do not do, but what I hate I do. And if I do what I do not want to do, I agree that the law is good. As it is, it is no longer I myself who do it, but it is sin living in me. For I know that good itself does not dwell in me, that is, in my sinful nature. For I have the desire to do what is good, but I cannot carry it out. For I do not do the good I want to do, but the evil I do not want to do—this I keep on doing. Now if I do what I do not want to do, it is no longer I who do it, but it is sin living in me that does it.

So I find this law at work: Although I want to do good, evil is right there with me. For in my inner being I delight in God's law; but I see another law at work in me, waging war against the law of my mind and making me a prisoner of the law of sin at work within me. What a wretched man I am! Who will rescue me from this body that is subject to death? Thanks be to God, who delivers me through Jesus Christ our Lord! So then, I myself in my mind am a slave to God's law, but in my sinful nature a slave to the law of sin (Rom 7:14–25).

I call this section *The Struggle of the Sinful Heart*. Paul began this passage by saying the law was *spiritual*. In what way? I believe the law is spiritual because it reveals for us the nature of God and His will for us—and God is *spiritual*. Our struggle is far more than a mere physical scuffle. As Paul detailed in Ephesians 6:12, our struggle is in the spiritual realm.

The verses are rather peculiar; one might say they are worded in a very Paul-like manner. But I think I might be able to offer you a simple clarification. Paul was speaking of our natural tendency to *not do right*. Even when we have the best intentions, we all fall in many ways and on many occasions. And it is for that very reason that the law is truly good. You might even call it a guardrail for a car that is prone to wander off the road. We are like that car that is prone to wander. Paul himself was honest enough to admit his natural tendency to sin. However, the law brought him back to the knowledge of the standard of God. The law revealed *right* and *wrong*. Otherwise, people would subjectively redefine right and wrong as they wish. Yet regardless of our natural tendencies, God's standard is ever constant.

Paul was also speaking of the limitation of the *goodness* of humanity. He was playing on the notion that even if people wanted to do good and fulfill the law, it was not within their capability to do so. Some might have been thinking about this in response to what Paul said back in 3:20, when he suggested that even if someone did all the law, he still would not be considered righteous. The caveat is that no one is capable of such an achievement. For a person to fulfill the whole law by his own efforts would mean a person could attain the standard of God on his own. Impossible. At this moment, you might be thinking about the Pharisees who were known for their unmatched righteousness. Jesus often pointed out how they were in fact righteous in many areas, but also neglected many areas at the same time. Why? Because of their human limitation. The standard of God is only attainable when He carries us by grace.

In these verses, Paul also revealed all the more how controlling the nature of sin is. He had pointed this out to us before, but he found it worth repeating. Paul understood that God was at work in him. But he also, while simply being honest with himself, knew that there was another law inside of him waging war. The struggle was a spiritual battle that a person will fight till their last breath. But while we struggle, may we make the same resolve that Paul did; I am a slave to God.

Our death to sin, through water baptism, broke the contractual bond between us and the law. We are now free to unite with Christ and the law of grace. We are free from the law, and we do not live under the law anymore. Yet, the law is quite useful. The law reveals the standards of God that have never changed. Consider just some of the basic things you know to be wrong: adultery, murder, lying, coveting, stealing, and so on. You know these are wrong because they are detailed in the law of God. Yet even the best of us are not capable to do all the good required in the law by our own efforts. But this is the very point; we are not good enough—we need Jesus.

Chapter Eight

It is a wonderful thing knowing that in Christ I am forgiven. But if we were only forgiven, what would be different than before? What would stop me from doing all the same things I did before? What would life be like if *all* you receive at the time of salvation was forgiveness? Peter said in Acts 2:38 that when we turn to Christ, we receive forgiveness, but also the gift of the Holy Spirit. The Holy Spirit is a helper given to us. The truth is, I need more than my sins forgiven; I need help living up to the standards of God. I need help being good.

Paul had adequately laid out the beautiful plan of salvation. Through the first seven chapters, we learned that we are all sinners who are incapable of earning any sort of righteousness on our own. With that, we were introduced to Jesus Christ who was sent to be our righteousness, to be our savior and atonement. However, as Abraham was declared righteous because of an active faith, we too will be declared righteous through an active faith. Paul showed us that a life in Christ means we must also have first died to our old life. We accomplish this through the act of obedience and faith while we are baptized into Christ.

Once people are baptized into Jesus Christ, they are Christians, but one most important ingredient is yet missing —we need help. During the last days Jesus was on the earth with His disciples, He promised to leave with them a helper, an advocate. Christ knows we cannot do this alone. The Holy Spirit is the presence of God that dwells inside of us. The Holy Spirit is a gift. Peter said in Acts 2:38, "Repent and be baptized, every one of you, in the name of Jesus Christ for the forgiveness of your sins. And you will receive the gift of the Holy Spirit." As much as I would love to expound on this promise, I must keep it simple and relevant to this chapter for now. We cannot do this on our own. We have a helper, the Holy Spirit transforming us day by day.

> Therefore, there is now no condemnation for those who are in Christ Jesus, because through Christ Jesus the law of the Spirit who gives life has set you free from the law of sin and death. For what the law was powerless to do because it was weakened by the flesh, God did by sending His own Son in the likeness of sinful flesh to be a sin offering. And so He condemned sin in the flesh, in order that the righteous requirement of the law might be fully met in us, who do not live according to the flesh but according to the Spirit (Rom 8:1–4).

Paul began by building from the last verse in chapter seven; "Thanks be to God, who delivers me through Jesus Christ our Lord!" —Where there is no condemnation. Paul was grateful for the work of Christ detailed in the previous chapters. And Paul knew that it was only the justification of Christ that could do such a feat.

Jesus and the law of the Spirit were able to set people free from sin. The law was not able to do that. The law was weakened. How could that be if the law was holy and perfect? There was no fault in the law, for the law did exactly as it was designed to do—it revealed sin. The law was powerless and weakened due to humanity's sin problem. God had always had a plan in Jesus Christ. But the plan was not only to forgive our sins. God's plan was also to provide a helper to guide us in this new life. *We do not live according to the flesh but according to the Spirit.* The Spirit is the gift of God. Now that I am forgiven and free from sin, the Spirit of God dwelling in me helps me to live holy.

> Those who live according to the flesh have their minds set on what the flesh desires; but those who live in accordance with the Spirit have their minds set on what the Spirit desires. The mind governed by the flesh is death, but the mind governed by the Spirit is life and peace. The mind governed by the flesh is hostile to God; it does not submit to God's law, nor can it do so. Those who are in the realm of the flesh cannot please God (Rom 8:5–8).

For the linguistic level Paul usually wrote at, this passage is as elementary as it gets. There are two different lives; one that follows after the flesh, and one that follows after the Spirit. It really depends on where we choose to put our minds. But we see the same thing we did in the latter part of chapter six; there are consequences to our decisions. If we choose to set our minds on the things of the flesh and be governed thereby, the consequence is death and hostility toward God. However, if we choose to be governed by the Spirit and set our minds on the things of the Spirit, the consequence is life and peace.

It really is a simple choice; anyone in his or her right mind would choose life and peace over death and hostility. However, we all know it is more difficult in practice. But that is the whole point of this chapter. Life is hard. By our own power we will continue to fall into the same traps of sin we always have. But if we allow the Holy Spirit to help, we can begin to move forward.

> You, however, are not in the realm of the flesh but are in the realm of the Spirit, if indeed the Spirit of God lives in you. And if anyone does not have the Spirit of Christ, they do not belong to Christ. But if Christ is in you, then even though your body is subject to death because of sin, the Spirit gives life because of righteousness. And if the Spirit of Him who raised Jesus from the dead is living in you, He who raised Christ from the dead will also give life to your mortal bodies because of His Spirit who lives in you (Rom 8:9–11).

The reason Paul said Christians are in the realm of the Spirit is that the Spirit of God dwells within us. The same was true when Paul called the law spiritual because it revealed the standards of God who is spiritual (7:14). And the only way to be in this realm is if we pass beyond the threshold and choose to follow Christ. When Paul spoke of the Spirit of God, he was speaking of the active nature of God on the earth. I have inserted an excerpt to further explain the Godhead:

* * *

An Elementary Exposition of the Distinction and Unity of the Godhead—The Father, Son, and Holy Spirit

I want to preface by stressing the complexity of what I am trying to accomplish. I am attempting to bring a simple and natural comprehension to something that is complex and spiritual. We only can begin to parse out the few gems God has sprinkled through His word. I believe that we must be content to accept that we cannot fully exhaust in these few pages the *fullness* of God. Therefore, I will lay out the Scriptures for you the best way I understand them, but in the end, I think it is healthy to conclude that God is simply too big for any of us to fully grasp. And simply said, I love that about Him. In this study, I will first show you the distinct features of each of the three persons of the Godhead. Then I will conclude by revealing their unity.

God the Father: When I think of *God*, I think of the central essence of the Godhead dwelling in heaven. When we look at the creation story, God uttered His voice from the cosmos. But it was His Spirit that formed the earth (Gen 1:1–2). When Jesus taught His disciples to pray, He said, "Our Father in heaven..." (Matt 6:9). Furthermore, when Jesus spoke of His departure, He said He was going to the Father (John 14:28). As you survey Scripture, you do not find *God the Father* coming in the flesh. His place is reserved in heaven while Jesus became the incarnate. *God the Father* does not dwell and move along the face of the earth; rather, this is distinctly the role of the Holy Spirit. There are a couple of times God did come within the atmosphere of earth, and nature quaked in His presence. We see this truth from God's visit with Moses on Mount Sinai (Exod 19:17–19), and also His visit with Elijah on Mount Horeb (1 Kgs 19:7–14. Where is God the Father? We see Him seated on his throne in heaven (Rev 4).

Jesus: John 1:1 says, "In the beginning was the Word, and the Word was with God, and the Word was God." Later in verse 14, we read that "the Word became flesh and made His dwelling among us." Jesus was the incarnate of God—God revealed in the flesh. Jesus was born into the flesh in 4 AD, but prior to that, He was with the Father. John was six months older than Jesus, yet he said that Jesus was *before* him (John 1:30). Jesus, speaking to the people said, "Before Abraham was born, I am" (John 8:58). And as we already read from John 1:1, Jesus was from the beginning. Where was He before He was born in 4 AD? He was with the Father in heaven. God *the Father* never has physically appeared on the earth. The Spirit of God has never been physically manifested. When God walked upon the earth, we called Him Jesus.

The Holy Spirit: Except for the incarnate of Jesus Christ, the only time God was presently active on the earth was through His *Spirit*. We see this very truth revealed in a host of Scriptures: In Genesis 1:1–2, it was the Spirit of God that hovered over the face of the earth; the Spirit was upon Moses and shared with the seventy elders (Num 11:25); The Holy Spirit was upon Joshua (Num 27:18), Othniel (Judg 3:10), Gideon (6:34), Samson (13:25; 14:6), and Saul (1 Sam 10:9–10); When David sinned and was afraid that God would leave him, he prayed, "Do not cast me from your presence or take your Holy Spirit from me" (Ps 51:11). When we come to the New Testament, we see the same truth. Even with the raising of Jesus, we gather that it was the Holy Spirit (Rom 8:11). And finally, on the day of Pentecost, we learn that those who were baptized in Christ were promised forgiveness of sins and the Holy Spirit dwelling in their hearts (Acts 2:38, Rom 8:11). Paul continued to speak of this active role of God in our lives through his letters, especially Galatians 5. The early Christians did not call this *God the Father*; He was on His throne in heaven to which they prayed. Nor did they think *Jesus the incarnate* was still with them; Jesus had gone to heaven to prepare a home. The gift to have God dwelling among His people was the Holy Spirit. The active presence of God on the earth, except for Jesus Christ for those few years, has always been the Holy Spirit.

The above has shown us the distinct roles of the three persons of the Godhead. Each role is very different from the other and rarely if ever do they overlap. Yet they are not three Gods. Some have referred to the three parts of an egg to help comprehend the separateness while being one. I contend that there is no human devise imaginable that could give us a perfect picture of the Godhead.

While the three are separate in function, they are the one God. Jesus gives us a remarkable image in John 14. When He spoke about the Holy Spirit, Jesus said, "Anyone who loves me will obey my teaching. My Father will love them, and we will come to them and make our home with them" (John 14:23). Notice the use of the *we*. The context in which Jesus was speaking was the promise

of the Holy Spirit, the Advocate. While promising the
Holy Spirit, Jesus spoke of Himself and the Father (we)
making Their home in those who obey the gospel. Let me
try to help us wrap our minds around this. Jesus made
claims that He was one with God (John 10:30; 14:9, 20;
17:11–23). The Hebrew writer spoke of Christ being the
exact representation of God (Heb 1:3). While at the same
time, we see a oneness with Christ and the Holy Spirit.
We saw above that the Holy Spirit is promised to dwell in
us once we obey (Acts 2:38, Rom 8:11). At the same time,
Paul speaks of *Christ in us* (Col 1:27). And in Ephesians
3:17, Paul spoke about Christ dwelling in our hearts.
While we see the Holy Spirit and Christ dwelling in us,
we also know from Paul's writings, that when we obey the
gospel, we are reconciled to God (Eph 4:2–4, 2 Cor
5:16–21). With perplexity, we realize that through obedience and faith, we are reconciled to every facet of God.

We often try to make a distinction with the members
of the Godhead. In role and function, we see a clear
purpose. But while noticing their distinct roles, one
would find it difficult to ignore the *oneness* at the same
time. Jesus said it well near the end of John's gospel: "*My
prayer is not for them alone. I pray also for those who will
believe in me through their message, that all of them may
be one, Father, just as you are in me and I am in you. May
they also be in us so that the world may believe that you
have sent me. I have given them the glory that you gave
me, that they may be one as we are one—I in them and you
in me—so that they may be brought to complete unity.
Then the world will know that you sent me and have loved
them even as you have loved me*" (John 17:20–23). Read
that passage slowly and it begins to come alive. God the

Father, Jesus, and the Holy Spirit are separate persons, yet They are one. We looked at many passages from the Bible, but I am inclined to think that none of the writers of the Bible fully understood this truth either. He is one God. Yet He functions in different ways. Maybe these *roles* of God are for our finite minds to help us understand what we really cannot. I continually find myself where Job was saying, "Surely I spoke of things I did not understand, things too wonderful for me to know" (Job 42:3b). And I am fine with not fully understanding God. I am fine with Him being bigger than my comprehension. That is the kind of God I will worship.

* * *

There is one reason God is able to dwell in us once we become Christians. As we saw in Acts 2:38, and also Romans 6, when we are baptized, our sins are washed away. It is at that moment that we died to sin. Because sin has been cleansed from us, God is able to come and dwell in us. Isaiah 59:1–2 reveals that there is one thing that separates us from God—sin. There has only been one thing; it has always been sin. That is why the only answer is Christ. The blood of Christ washes my sins away.

I could never fully wrap my mind around verse 11. Paul spoke of the *Spirit that raised Jesus from the dead.* That is the Holy Spirit. That is the same Spirit that hovered over the face of the earth during creation (Gen 1:2). He hovered over the emptiness and void, and when God gave the command, the Spirit created. Yes, *that* Spirit! Living in me. I don't think we can fully comprehend this. And might I add, it is only by God's grace that we can even handle it. I realize that God wants to create as He did several thousand years ago. But not the worlds; now He wants to move in my heart. David understood this when he prayed, "*Create* in me a pure heart, O God..." (Ps 51:10a). To have the God of the universe, the God who created the universe, living in me—there is something about that is both terrifying and amazing at the same time.

In this last verse of the passage, we also found our source of life. As we saw in chapters six and seven, we died. We died to sin—nonetheless, we died. But after the fashion of the resurrection of Christ, we were raised up into a newness of life. But what is the source of that life? God Himself, specifically His Spirit. My life is through God, and in Him and only in Him am I alive. I am not talking about physical life but being alive spiritually—truly being alive. I was dead, but now I live—I live because He lives. I live because He is in me.

> Therefore, brothers and sisters, we have an obligation—but it is not to the flesh, to live according to it. For if you live according to the flesh, you will die; but if by the Spirit you put to death the misdeeds of the body, you will live. For those who are led by the Spirit of God are the children of God. The Spirit you received does not make you slaves, so that you live in fear again; rather, the Spirit you received brought about your adoption to sonship. And by Him we cry, "*Abba,* Father." The Spirit himself testifies with our spirit that we are God's children. Now if we are children, then we are heirs—heirs of God and co-heirs with Christ, if indeed we share in His sufferings in order that we may also share in His glory (Rom 8:12–17).

Paul suggested that we have an obligation. Now I know that as soon as the word *obligation* is mentioned, many might lose interest. And that is why Paul took a moment to talk about it. People in the time of Paul were not too much different than today. Paul said we have an obligation to live according to the Spirit and put away the deeds of the flesh.

Paul was challenging the idea that some likely had, and some still today, and that is that Christianity is a form of slavery. That doesn't sound attractive. Not quite the sales pitch you would give to lead someone to Christ. Paul considered himself a slave to God in view of his service to God, but when you look at Paul's comments on Christianity, he gave a different tone. In this passage, Paul encouraged the church in Rome not to look at Christianity as slavery, but as *adoption*. And as adopted children of God, Paul helped them to understand the value. He was encouraging them not to focus on what they felt they were lacking while being a Christian, but rather look at the benefits they gain in their adoption. He named just a few at that time: heirs with God and co-heirs with Christ. And if they choose to follow a life in Christ, they will share in His glory. Now that is a sales pitch. Heir to the Creator of the universe. That is simply unreal. If I have to lay down a few deeds of the flesh that are not good for me anyway, is it not more than worth it? If you put the two choices on a scale, they don't even come close. Living in Christ is far better.

I consider that our present sufferings are not worth comparing with the glory that will be revealed in us. For the creation waits in eager expectation for the children of God to be revealed. For the creation was subjected to frustration, not by its own choice, but by the will of the one who subjected it, in hope that the creation itself will be liberated from its bondage to decay and brought into the freedom and glory of the children of God. We know that the whole creation has been groaning as in the pains of childbirth right up to the present time. Not only so, but we ourselves, who have the firstfruits of the Spirit, groan inwardly as we wait eagerly for our adoption to sonship, the redemption of our bodies. For in this hope we were saved. But hope that is seen is no hope at all. Who hopes for what they already have? But if we hope for what we do not yet have, we wait for it patiently (Rom 8:18–25).

The previous section introduced the idea that as we are heirs with Christ, we will also share in His sufferings. However, if we share in His sufferings, we will also share in His glory. In this new section, Paul will add to that thought. Many might have thought that they would love to share in God's glory, but would rather forgo the suffering. The suffering we are speaking of was spoken of in chapter five. The suffering that produces perseverance and leads to character and gives hope. But still, suffering is suffering, and no one wants to suffer. Paul shared in this section that the suffering we may experience will not compare to the glory that will be revealed in us. In essence, Paul was saying it will be well worth it. It is always hard to see this in the moment of suffering, but if we endure, we will see.

I want to take a closer look at the end of verse 18. Paul spoke of the glory that will be revealed *in us*. With that, we should understand that he was not talking about the glory of our future home in heaven, nor was he speaking of the glory of God Himself. He was speaking of the glory *in us*. Remember, this chapter introduced the work of the Holy Spirit in our lives. God wants to transform us day by day. Sometimes we will face suffering, but the end goal is that the work of God in us will produce something amazing and be a testimony unto the Lord—Paul called this *glory*. And he said that even though we may suffer some, the glory of God's work in our lives and what He is doing in us far outweighs the cost.

Verses 19–25 are rather complicated, and commentaries vary greatly with their interpretations. I believe Paul was paralleling our relationship with God to the balance of nature itself. Simply said, we are all designed by God to be His children. And it seems that creation was built around that union. And when we are separated from God, creation is at unrest. Is this how it really works? We are not really sure; I would assume not. But the point that Paul was stressing is the utmost and paramount desire of God to draw us back to Himself in adoption. And Paul was using an analogy from creation to show that when humanity is separated from God, it is against the natural order in which God created everything.

Not only is nature at unrest, but Paul said that *we* are at unrest when we are apart from God. Paul said our very bodies *groan inwardly as we wait eagerly for our adoption to sonship, the redemption of our bodies.* I can't really explain what this means or how this works in reality. But again, we must look at the point. We are designed to be children of God, adopted sons and daughters. Somehow, someway, whether we are aware of it or not, our bodies long to be a child of God. And our hope is that we find this rest and salvation in God. Creation is at unrest. Our bodies are at unrest. God designed us to be near to Him. When Paul wrote this, I imagine he had in mind the scene of Adam and Eve walking in the cool of the day with God. Such union and peace. But that all ended with sin. We cannot return to the garden, but God does want us to return to Him.

> In the same way, the Spirit helps us in our weakness. We do not know what we ought to pray for, but the Spirit Himself intercedes for us through wordless groans. And He who searches our hearts knows the mind of the Spirit, because the Spirit intercedes for God's people in accordance with the will of God (Rom 8:26–27).

This can be a difficult passage; furthermore, commentaries hardly agree on its interpretation. I hope to offer clarity. I think the first thing we must do is understand that this passage is speaking about something that happens between the Holy Spirit and God. Our part is to pray. But then, the Holy Spirit intercedes for us. This is far outside of our league or involvement.

When I read this passage understanding that this is something between the Holy Spirit and God, I realize that my prayer is *more* than mere words that enter an empty atmosphere. I believe that may be Paul's point. The picture we are given is that the Holy Spirit is alongside us as we pray. And sometimes when we pray, we stumble with our words and we say the wrong thing, and sometimes we simply do not know what to say. The Holy Spirit intercedes. And while we sometimes might think that our prayer was ineffective and not heard by God, the promise is that the Holy Spirit intercedes. The picture we have is that the Holy Spirit takes our prayer, as messy as it might be, and He stands before God with it and speaks on our behalf. You might say He is like a lawyer. That might be why Jesus said of the Holy Spirit, "If you love me, keep my commands. And I will ask the Father, and He will give you another advocate to help you and be with you forever—the Spirit of truth (John 14:15–17a).

Some have mistakenly taken this passage to support speaking in tongues. But I contend that this passage cannot possibly be used to support speaking in tongues as it says the Holy Spirit intercedes through *wordless groans*. It is clear that this phenomenon is neither *seen* nor *heard* in the physical realm. Again, this intercession is a divine event between the Holy Spirit and God.

Upon our salvation, we have been given a helper, the Holy Spirit. He *brings life*. He *transforms*. And He *intercedes*. This would have been great news for the early church. During those hard days as the church was growing in the midst of persecution, things were going to be okay. How did they know? Because God was with them. This leads us to our next section.

> And we know that in all things God works for the good of those who love Him, who have been called according to His purpose. For those God foreknew He also predestined to be conformed to the image of His Son, that He might be the firstborn among many brothers and sisters. And those He predestined, He also called; those He called, He also justified; those He justified, He also glorified (Rom 8:28–30).

Some have used this passage in error in several ways. I wish not to delve into those ways but only to unveil what I believe is the truth. When we look at these verses in their context, we will find that they are filled with life. To properly understand the message Paul is trying to relay, we must notice the climax of *glory*. So, what I would like to do is work backward from glory and see if we can recreate the original thought of Paul.

Glorified: The finale, the end of the matter, is to be glorified. Paul was feeding off the previous idea he started in 8:18. The desire of God is that He might be glorified in our lives. But there are things that precede glory. One thing Paul states that must precede glory is *justification*.

Justified: Before the Lord is glorified in our lives, we must be justified. Paul was feeding from 3:21–31. Paul stated very clearly that we are not justified on our own nor by any of our best efforts. But in 3:26, Paul introduced Christ as the one who is *just* and the *justifier*. God takes our wrongdoings and makes them right through the atonement of His Son. This must take place before glory. Both justification and glory are what we were created for (8:18–25).

Called: People cannot attain justification and glory on their own, they must first be called by God; one might even say *invited*. I appreciate the Parable of the Wedding Banquet in Matthew 22:1–14. At first, the banquet is only for a particular group. This would be referring to the Jews through the Old Testament. However, as the parable goes on, many of the invited do not come. So, the master sends the servant to go invite all and any he could find. The invitation is for all. God has called *everyone*. Paul continued to explain that God has called everyone He has *predestined*.

Predestined: To be predestined is the same idea to be determined beforehand. Paul said that those God had determined beforehand to be saved, He called, and those who were called, He justified, and those He justified, He glorified. Some have limited the grace of God to think that God has only called a certain number of people. But what does the text say: Who did God predestine? Those he *foreknew*.

Foreknow: It is as simple as it sounds; to foreknow means to know beforehand. If you believe that God is eternal and all-knowing, you should come to the same conclusion as I have—God has foreknown *everyone*. There is no simpler truth to be told in this entire book. There is no person God has not known beforehand.

It is as simple as this: God has foreknown *everyone*. Therefore, He has predestined *everyone* to be conformed to His image. Therefore, He has called, or invited, *everyone*. Therefore, He has the desire to justify *everyone*. And to return to the climax, God wants to be glorified in the life of *everyone*.

Loved: We must not forget the *why*. Why has God done all this and desired us in such a way? Verse 28 gives us the answer; because of His love for us. And the person who responds to such a pursuing love is promised good from God.

> What, then, shall we say in response to these things? If God is for us, who can be against us? He who did not spare His own Son, but gave Him up for us all—how will He not also, along with Him, graciously give us all things? Who will bring any charge against those whom God has chosen? It is God who justifies. Who then is the one who condemns? No one. Christ Jesus who died—more than that, who was raised to life—is at the right hand of God and is also interceding for us. Who shall separate us from the love of Christ? Shall trouble or hardship or persecution or famine or nakedness or danger or sword? As it is written: "For your sake we face death all day long; we are considered as sheep to be slaughtered." No, in all these

things we are more than conquerors through Him who
loved us. For I am convinced that neither death nor life,
neither angels nor demons, neither the present nor the
future, nor any powers, neither height nor depth, nor
anything else in all creation, will be able to separate us
from the love of God that is in Christ Jesus our Lord
(Rom 8:31–39).

This passage reveals the point Paul had been trying to
convey all along—God is for us. The rest of the passage
builds on this very truth. What is life like when God is for
you? First, Paul mentioned that God has chosen us, therefore
who can bring any charge? Secondly, he said God justifies
us, therefore who can bring any condemnation? Finally, with
God for us, no one can separate us from the love of God.
With that in the mind of Paul, he ended the passage stressing
just how powerful the love of God is.

While we look at this passage and stand amazed at the
boundless love of God, we must not forget the whole counsel
of God. Without minimizing the love of God, there is in fact
one thing that Paul mentioned that can separate us from
God—our sin. And it is for that very reason that God sent
Jesus to take our sins upon the cross.

There has been much confusion over these verses and
how they are interpreted. There are ideologies that believe
these verses mean that once you are in Christ, absolutely
nothing can take you away. And that is so true; there is
nothing that can take us from the love of God. God's love
will always be there. God's love was demonstrated to us
while we were sinners. But Paul made it very clear that we
are slaves to whom we obey. We have to make a choice to
yield to God. Once I am in Christ, it is true, sin and all the

forces of hell have no power over me. But I have to make a daily choice to follow Christ. Whether we sin or walk in righteousness, that does not change the love of God for us one bit. God's love, unlike ours, is ever constant. However, we have to choose to stay faithful to Him.

Paul had spent the last few chapters looking at the fundamentals of salvation. And although Paul showed us the beauty of turning to Christ in faith, choosing to be baptized into Jesus, and dying to our sinful nature, Paul also wanted us to know that there is a whole new life after. The life after we turn to Christ is new and we live in Christ. Our new life is lived for God and with the help of the Holy Spirit. And if we yield to the plan of God to make us His workmanship, great things will happen.

If you were to look through the whole of Scripture, you will find something true about the Holy Spirit. From the garden of Eden to the days of Moses, Joshua, and many others, you see a common truth. Even to the raising of Jesus Christ, there has been a common truth that we must not miss. Where God is actively working on the earth revealing His power and presence, we have always called that His Spirit. When we turn to Christ and are baptized, Paul shared with us from chapter eight that God—the Holy Spirit —wants to dwell with us.

This new life in Christ cannot be lived alone—we were not meant to do it alone. God provided a helper. The Christian life is to walk in the presence of the Holy Spirit of God who strengthens, encourages, and works in our hearts.

Interlude

We are at a breakpoint in the book of Romans. As we will see in chapters nine to the end, Paul completely changed gears from the first eight chapters. This interlude is designed to help us understand what we just looked at in the last eight chapters. In short, Paul brought the reader from being lost in sin to becoming a Spirit-filled forgiven Christian with a new life. Through these first eight chapters, we must not miss the *how*. How does a person get from being lost in sin to becoming a Christian? The following are practical steps laid out by Paul and also shadowed throughout the book of Acts. I believe if you follow these steps, you will become a Christian in the same manner as they did in the first-century church.

Believe: Paul said he was not ashamed of the gospel because it "is the power of God that brings salvation to everyone who *believes*" (Rom 1:16). It should go without saying that one must believe, but it is a present first step in the book of Romans. We have seen above that *faith* and

believing are the same word in Greek. Romans 3:22 speaks
of a righteousness that is by *faith*. Also in 5:1, Paul said that
Christians are justified by *faith*. The very first step is faith—
to believe. But faith is not the finish line, rather it prompts a
person to respond to God. Paul spoke of his ministry as one
who was sent to "call all the Gentiles to the *obedience* that
comes from faith for His name's sake" (1:5). Faith prompts
action. Faith prompts obedience. The question one should
ask at this point is, *what do I do to be obedient?*

Confess Jesus as Lord: although Paul did not explicitly
say in the first eight chapters that one has to confess, he did
clearly say it in 10:13. In chapter 6, Paul spoke of the Christian life as being one no longer enslaved by sin. In the last
half of the chapter, Paul spoke of the choice each person has
to choose who his or her lord will be. He encouraged the
Christians not to yield themselves to sin and not to let sin
reign in their body. Furthermore, Paul warned them that
they were slaves to the one they chose to obey. The people
had a fork in the road; they had to choose who their lord
would be. Paul wrote in 6:17, "But thanks be to God that,
though you used to be slaves to sin, you have come to obey
from your heart the pattern of teaching that has now claimed
your allegiance." Being free from sin, they were now free to
make Jesus Lord.

Repentance: The definition of repentance is simple: *to
turn around, to change direction.* Paul began the letter by
pointing out the one problem that must be addressed—sin.
The last half of chapter one details the grotesque image of a
society lost in wretched sin. In chapter two, Paul clarified
that there was nothing people could do to change that on
their own; people could not remove sin on their own, and
could not live without sinning. And since sin is the one thing

that separates people from God (Isa 59:1–2), a remedy is imperative. In the latter half of chapter three, Paul introduced the saving grace of Jesus Christ and the washing away of sin. When considering the amazing grace of God, Paul asked a rhetorical question; "Shall we go on sinning so that grace may increase (6:1)? His answer was obvious. The reason Paul gave is that a Christian is one who should be dead to sin. In verse 2, Paul continued to say, "We are those who have died to sin." To choose a life in Christ, a person must choose to make Him Lord. And as Master, God demands a change of lifestyle. As we will see soon, not only does He demand it, but He also helps from within through the Holy Spirit.

Baptism in water: There is a point in time, one might say a threshold, in which a person is cleansed from his sin; when a person is a new creation. Paul said it is at the point of baptism. Paul said in the early verses of chapter 6, "All of us who were baptized into Christ Jesus were baptized into his death" (6:3). It is at this time that our sinful nature dies. Remember, it is our sin that separates us from God. Therefore, it is impossible to be any closer to God until our sin is dealt with. At baptism, our old nature was put to death. However, we did not die to our old nature for no reason; we died that we might be alive, as we read in 6:4. Anyone who claims to have eternal life had to receive it as a gift from God. That gift of life comes from our physical baptism which symbolizes the death, burial, and resurrection of Christ. Peter also clarified this on the day of Pentecost when saying, "Repent and be baptized, every one of you, in the name of Jesus Christ for the forgiveness of your sins. And you will receive the gift of the Holy Spirit" (Acts 2:38). Baptism is an important act of obedience that is prompted by faith. In the early church, when people chose to become Christians, they were baptized that same day.

The Holy Spirit: Without help, we would wander back into the same sinful pit we were in before we chose to follow Christ. But God dwells in us and transforms us. As we read in Acts 2:38, the Holy Spirit is a promise given to those who were baptized in water. In Romans chapter eight, Paul brought us to the culmination of becoming a Christian—having the Spirit of God dwell within your heart. The Spirit breathed life into us whereas sin only brought death. Paul said, "if the Spirit of him who raised Jesus from the dead is living in you, He who raised Christ from the dead will also give life to your mortal bodies because of His Spirit who lives in you" (8:11). That is fascinating and terrifying at the same time. There is only one Spirit of God. The same Spirit that raised Jesus from the dead. The same Spirit that hovered over the face of the waters in Genesis two during creation. That Spirit! He wants to dwell in our hearts. He wants to comfort us. He wants to guide us. He wants to transform us. Paul calls this *living by the Spirit*. It is life.

* * *

That is the journey from being lost in sin to becoming a Spirit-filled and forgiven Christian.

1. Believe in God and Jesus Christ.
2. Confess Jesus as Lord.
3. Repent of your sins.
4. Be baptized in water.
5. Receive the Holy Spirit.

When you rise up out of the water, as Peter promised, you rise up with your sins washed away and given the promised Holy Spirit. Writing to the Corinthians, Paul said you are a *new creation* (2 Cor 5:17). To the Romans, he wrote of being adopted by God (8:15). Therein is eternal life.

Chapter Nine

The train of thought we have read during the first eight chapters has come to an end. As Paul begins chapter nine, not necessarily changing topics, he changes the tone. Paul took us on a marvelous salvific crescendo as he took us from being lost sinners to Spirit-filled Christians in just eight chapters. The climax was truly in chapter eight with the same Spirit that raised Christ from the dead living in us giving us life. But now the tone changes as Paul had to address something on his heart. When Paul came to the end of chapter eight, imagine with me the excitement and intensity in Paul's mind as he was writing this letter. He was telling the church in Rome that in Christ and living in the Spirit, they were more than conquerors. And absolutely nothing could separate them from the love of God. Then imagine Paul finishing that sentence and beginning the next verses that we would come to know as 9:1. Paul's demeanor changed drastically. What was joy and excitement was now dim and concerning. There was something heavy on the heart of Paul that needed to be addressed.

So, with sadness in his heart, he placed the pen to the paper again. This time, not to build to a Spirit-filled salvation, but to express his concern for the lost Jews.

> I speak the truth in Christ—I am not lying, my conscience
> confirms it through the Holy Spirit—I have great sorrow
> and unceasing anguish in my heart. For I could wish that
> I myself were cursed and cut off from Christ for the sake
> of my people, those of my own race (Rom 9:1–3).

The way Paul began this passage indicates that he may have been responding to an accusation from others saying he abandoned his ancestry for his new-found religion. Paul responded by telling them that his heart yearned for them. He had sorrow for his own people. Although Paul and the church in Rome had decided to follow Christ, many Jews did not come to that decision yet. It seemed evident that Paul would do anything to change this. In fact, what more could a person ask of Paul? He gave his life over to the gospel, suffering tortures of all sorts, being shipwrecked more than once, and so much more. Why? So he could reach as many as possible (1 Cor 9:19). To the fullest, Paul was trying to follow the example of Christ. He had a fervent heart for the lost. For Paul to live, it was for the cause of Christ.

> The people of Israel. Theirs is the adoption to sonship;
> theirs the divine glory, the covenants, the receiving of the
> law, the temple worship and the promises. Theirs are the
> patriarchs, and from them is traced the human ancestry
> of the Messiah, who is God over all, forever praised!
> Amen (Rom 9:4–5).

Paul was astonished and saddened by how much the Jews had been given, just to end up missing the main thing. Furthermore, Paul refused to speak poorly about the heritage of the Jews. He contended that they had been given many good things from God: they were given adoption to sonship, they were given divine glory, they were given the covenants, they were given the law, they were given the temple worship, they were given the promises, and they were given the patriarchs from which is traced the human ancestry of the Messiah. Remember from 3:1–2, Paul argued that there was an advantage to being a Jew. The list just mentioned shares a few of the advantages.

Though there were many advantages to being a Jew, and though they were given so much, Paul was saddened that they missed the culmination of the plan of God. Everything they were given was intended to lead and point them to the one thing they rejected—Jesus. Paul was concerned for them because they were refusing to be a part of the unfolding plan of God to redeem all people. The Jews had been a part of the unfolding plan of God for more than a thousand years. And now that it culminated with the Redeemer arriving to save everyone, they rejected Him. For this Paul had sorrow.

The following section (verses 6–29) should be taken as a whole, but we will also take a moment to digest each individually. Chapter nine was brilliantly written by Paul with bookends that provide us with the subject of the whole chapter—Paul's concern for his fellow Jews in their disbelief. But specifically, Paul wanted to show that God's plan did not fail.

In the following section between the two bookends, Paul is going to provide five illustrations that he will pull from the Old Testament that will help the reader understand his point. Each of the illustrations will push primarily two ideas: first, Paul is going to show that the Jews were not chosen based on their physical decent, but upon promise and election; secondly, Paul wanted them to understand that just as God chose the Jews, He can choose others as well—the Gentiles.

Illustration #1

> It is not as though God's word had failed. For not all who are descended from Israel are Israel. Nor because they are His descendants are they all Abraham's children. On the contrary, "It is through Isaac that your offspring will be reckoned." In other words, it is not the children by physical descent who are God's children, but it is the children of the promise who are regarded as Abraham's offspring. For this was how the promise was stated: "At the appointed time I will return, and Sarah will have a son." (Rom 9:6–9)

The first illustration was taken from Genesis 18:1–14; Abraham and Sarah. The point Paul was trying to make here was that the Jews were children of promise, not ethnicity. He began the passage by referring to "God's word." What was Paul referring to? I believe he was referring to all the promises spoken of in verses 4–5. These were God's promises that were spoken toward the Jews. Because the Jews had rejected the plan of redemption, does that mean God's word had failed?

God's word has never failed. To justify his answer, Paul brought forward a point from the story of Abraham and

Sarah; the simple fact that Abraham had more than only one child. This would mean realistically that the promise was not about physical descent, for that would mean all the children of Ishmael, the half-brother to Isaac, were heirs of the promise as well. And I am sure that every Jew did not support that notion. But that means they could not simply claim the promises because they were sons of Abraham, and this was the very point Paul was trying to make. Therefore, the descent of Abraham was not the answer that merited salvation. This would have triggered their interest. Many, if not all, claimed the promises just because they were sons of Abraham. They were now forced to wonder what the promises were all about.

Illustration #2

> Not only that, but Rebekah's children were conceived at the same time by our father Isaac. Yet, before the twins were born or had done anything good or bad—in order that God's purpose in election might stand: not by works but by him who calls—she was told, "The older will serve the younger." Just as it is written: "Jacob I loved, but Esau I hated." (Rom 9:10–13)

In this second illustration, Paul used the story of Jacob and Esau from Genesis 25:21–26. The point Paul will make is that the Jews were children of *election* and not of *works*. Paul had to address a tradition that has seeped deep into Jewish theology, teaching them that they were justified and chosen because of their works. The story in Genesis was about how God chose Jacob over Esau even before they were able to prove themselves by any works; therefore, it was by election. Paul's argument was that the Jews were chosen by God in the same manner; they were chosen by election, rather than their ethnicity, their works, or even that they were children of Abraham. This also took away all room for boasting which he also addressed in 3:27–31. The point was that they did not and could not earn their righteousness. They were elected by God not because of their goodness, but because of His grace.

Illustration #3

What then shall we say? Is God unjust? Not at all! For He says to Moses, "I will have mercy on whom I have mercy, and I will have compassion on whom I have compassion." It does not, therefore, depend on human desire or effort, but on God's mercy (Rom 9:14–16).

Paul used a statement God made to Moses in Exodus 33:19–20. What we must understand from Paul's point is that God did not act unjustly; rather, humanity does not deserve *any* good thing from God. I am reminded of the parable of the workers in the vineyard (Matt 20:1–16). This was a parable about the justice of God. The vineyard owner paid the first worker the fair wage they agreed on. Out of his mercy, the owner chose to pay the other workers the same, although they worked fewer hours. The point is that God can show mercy and compassion to anyone He wishes. From the previous illustration, the Jews would have realized they were chosen by election, not by merit. The idea that they would start to see is that God did not choose them because of *their* goodness, but because of His goodness, mercy, and compassion. And to press the point, God can show that mercy to anyone He wants, even to the Gentiles.

The Jews had to realize that they were shown a great deal of mercy. But they had to understand that they were not saved by heritage or works. They were chosen because of the goodness of God. Paul was trying to help the Jews see that God wanted to show that same mercy and goodness to the rest of the world.

Illustration #4

> For Scripture says to Pharaoh: "I raised you up for this very purpose, that I might display my power in you and that my name might be proclaimed in all the earth." Therefore God has mercy on whom He wants to have mercy, and He hardens whom He wants to harden (Rom 9:17–18).

Paul addressed the idea of some being raised with a special purpose and others having hardened hearts. The illustration he used is that of Pharaoh, who hardened his heart during the days of Moses (Ex 9:13–19). Keep in mind that the Jews thought they were special and that they had earned their special role. When we look at those with hard hearts in Scripture, we realize that God did not harden the heart of any person who did not already set his feet on the wrong path. We see this clearly in both the story of Pharaoh and Judas. God often has the bigger picture in mind whereas we are very *now* centered. In this context, it was the Jews who had their hearts hardened by God. They too had previously set their feet on stubbornly rejecting Jesus. However, Paul will say later that God hardened their hearts to stir the Gentiles to jealousy. What is the big picture? In chapter eleven, after the number of Jews respond, God will draw the Jews back in. As we will see in that chapter, it is not about exclusion, but about inclusion—as many as the Lord can save.

Illustration #5

> One of you will say to me: "Then why does God still blame us? For who is able to resist His will?" But who are you, a human being, to talk back to God? "Shall what is formed say to the one who formed it, 'Why did you make me like this?'" Does not the potter have the right to make out of the same lump of clay some pottery for special purposes and some for common use? (Rom 9:19–21)

The final illustration used by Paul comes from Jeremiah 18:1–10. Paul mentioned the idea of the potter and the clay. The passage above may seem a little harsh, perhaps like God is mean and unfair. But a good perspective to have is to consider the question, *what other created things complain or even have the ability to complain about its design?* Consider a rock, a tree, or any animal; all do not have the ability to complain. But humanity does.

God created humanity with the ability to reason, fabricate, and imagine. These are blessings in our design that no other creature was given, at least to this degree. I guess to get to the point—God created us in His image and with the ability to think. I venture to say that God does not wish that a person turn and uses his God-given imagination against his own Creator. Nor does God have to give a reason for His design and plan and justify anything He does. Yet humanity, in its haughtiness, often challenges God as being equal. We are the clay; God is the Potter.

The reason Paul ended with this illustration is that it brought it all to a close. The first four illustrations were Paul's *reasoning* with the people to help them understand the rationale of the plan of God. This final illustration was down to the point. *I am the Potter. You are the clay. I know it doesn't sound nice, but I don't have to justify my actions.* But they would have also remembered that just a few verses ago in 8:28, Paul said that God wanted to do good things for them that love Him. It really comes down to trust. The Jews may not have understood what God's design was, but God was asking them to simply trust Him as the good Potter.

All of these illustrations given by Paul had a common theme: they were designed to help us understand what God was doing and also how God thinks. For the church in Rome, these illustrations were meant to help them understand that God was adding the Gentiles. This was the mystery of the gospel that we will see in the next section.

What if God, although choosing to show His wrath and make His power known, bore with great patience the objects of His wrath—prepared for destruction? What if He did this to make the riches of His glory known to the objects of His mercy, whom He prepared in advance for glory—even us, whom He also called, not only from the Jews but also from the Gentiles? As He says in Hosea: "I

will call them 'my people' who are not my people; and I
will call her 'my loved one' who is not my loved one," and,
"In the very place where it was said to them, 'You are not
my people,' there they will be called 'children of the
living God.'" Isaiah cries out concerning Israel: "Though
the number of the Israelites be like the sand by the sea,
only the remnant will be saved. For the Lord will carry
out His sentence on earth with speed and finality." It is
just as Isaiah said previously: "Unless the Lord Almighty
had left us descendants, we would have become like
Sodom, we would have been like Gomorrah." (Rom
9:22–29)

Who are the objects of mercy and the objects of God's
wrath? This would have been clear in the minds of both the
Jews and the Gentiles in the early church. The Jews would
have likely thought that they were the objects of mercy. We
saw earlier in this chapter all the blessings the Jews were
given. They truly were recipients of God's mercy. That
would mean the Gentiles were the objects of God's wrath.
The question that Paul wanted to put in the minds of the
Jews is, *what if God wanted to show mercy to those objects of
wrath?* God wanted to show His mercy to the Jews *and* the
Gentiles. Sadly, we will see the tables turn as we get into
chapter eleven; because of disbelief, the Jews became the
objects of God's wrath. But even then, God was ready to
mercifully graft them back into the kingdom if they returned.

Paul used several verses from the Old Testament to
support his point. The Jews held the Scriptures in high
regard. Using a handful of Scriptures, Paul showed that even
the prophets spoke of God calling a people His own who
were not His own—the Gentiles. They would have seen that

the plan was always full inclusion as we will also see in chapter eleven.

> What then shall we say? That the Gentiles, who did not pursue righteousness, have obtained it, a righteousness that is by faith; but the people of Israel, who pursued the law as the way of righteousness, have not attained their goal. Why not? Because they pursued it not by faith but as if it were by works. They stumbled over the stumbling stone. As it is written: "See, I lay in Zion a stone that causes people to stumble and a rock that makes them fall, and the one who believes in Him will never be put to shame." (Rom 9:30–33)

Time has a way of changing how we see things. The law never was intended to be salvation. Circumcision was made by the Jews into a rite of passage, thinking that if you were circumcised, you were righteous, and if not, you were damned. But circumcision was designed to be a sign of the work God had done in them. The Jews made the law a requirement to fulfill in order to be considered holy. But the law was designed to reveal what sin was and show the people what God's will was for their lives. The Old Testament sacrifices and the law never had the power to save and make holy. The Jews were taking the gifts of God and making them into something attainable by works. By doing this, the Jews were missing out on the greatest gift God has ever given—their salvation through Jesus Christ, the culmination of the law.

Back to the point that this whole chapter was meant to convey, Paul's heart was aching for his fellow Jews that had rejected Jesus Christ. Paul had such compassion for his brothers that he would choose to be cut off from Christ if it meant their salvation. He pleaded with the Jews trying to show them that God desired to save everyone, but it must be through Christ. Paul will continue this thought in chapter ten as he begins by saying that his one desire is that they may be saved. But not everyone will accept the good news.

Chapter Ten

P aul changed his tone in chapter nine; he spent the first half of the letter (chs. 1–8) discussing the intricate plan of salvation. In chapter nine, Paul began to address the concern he had for the Jews who had rejected the message of Christ. It is very clear from the text that Paul would have done anything to see his fellow Jews turn to Christ and return to the fulfilled plan of God for them. As we now go into chapter ten, we will see Paul continue this concern for the Jews. He will praise them for their zeal, but he will also communicate his concern for their lack of knowledge. Paul would continue to share with them that the plan of God culminated in Christ, and it is only through Him and by His name that they will see the salvation of God.

Brothers and sisters, my heart's desire and prayer to God for the Israelites is that they may be saved. For I can testify about them that they are zealous for God, but their zeal is not based on knowledge. Since they did not know the righteousness of God and sought to establish their

own, they did not submit to God's righteousness. Christ is
the culmination of the law so that there may be righteousness for everyone who believes (Rom 10:1–4).

I want to bring our attention back to the thought I first
presented back in chapter five; it is best to view the plan of
salvation as a *linear* set of events unfolding over a timeline
set by God. Therefore, one of the points Paul was making is
that God did not abandon that plan—rather it is still unfolding. The problem Paul presented here was that the Jews
were rejecting the most important and culminating part of
the plan—Jesus Christ.

Paul began this chapter as he did chapter nine; with a
plea to his fellow Jews. But remember, the original writing
was a letter with no chapter breaks. So, it might be best to
ignore the "chapter 10" break and treat this as the same
thought Paul had from chapter nine. Paul's heart was aching
for his fellow Jews, and he wished they would be saved.

In the passage at hand, Paul praised the Jews for their
zeal. They stood firm on the law of Moses and took their religion very seriously. However, their zeal was not based on
knowledge. Consider the crucifixion of Christ; the Jews were
full of zeal as they demanded this blasphemous imposter be
crucified. Of course, we know they lacked much knowledge.
Consider Paul when he was Saul of Tarsus; he hunted
Christians down while trying to preserve the Jewish faith.
The Jews were known for their zeal, and that was praiseworthy. But they lacked knowledge.

The text reveals specifically what knowledge the Jews
lacked; the righteousness of God. The Jews had strayed from
the original intent of the law as we also detailed in chapter
five. On many occasions, through the letters of Paul, he had

to address the Jew's efforts to become righteous by doing the law. At first glance this makes sense; do the law=righteousness. However, to think so simplistically would be to say there is only a small gap between humanity and God—so small that we are able to span the difference with our efforts. Such is not the case.

The law of God was given for one purpose; to reveal the standard and nature of God. However, the Jews' rationale, whether spoken or not, was to assume that people were able to be like God and maintain his standard. Again, such an assumption implies that God is not so different from what we are. Furthermore, His ways are attainable by our efforts. But there is nothing in the above statement that is true. The law was never intended to save. Paul was trying to get them to return to the plan of God which was unfolding and culminating in Jesus Christ who was to be their righteousness.

> Moses writes this about the righteousness that is by the law: "The person who does these things will live by them." But the righteousness that is by faith says: "Do not say in your heart, 'Who will ascend into heaven?'" (that is, to bring Christ down) "or 'Who will descend into the deep?'" (that is, to bring Christ up from the dead). But what does it say? "The word is near you; it is in your mouth and in your heart," that is, the message concerning faith that we proclaim: If you declare with your mouth, "Jesus is Lord," and believe in your heart that God raised Him from the dead, you will be saved. For it is with your heart that you believe and are justified, and it is with your mouth that you profess your faith and are saved. As Scripture says, "Anyone who believes in Him will never be put to shame." For there is no difference between Jew

and Gentile—the same Lord is Lord of all and richly blesses all who call on Him, for, "Everyone who calls on the name of the Lord will be saved." (Rom 10:5–13)

This passage is most common for the often-quoted verse about calling on the name of the Lord. Paul began by showing us what Moses had to say about the law (Lev 18:5; Deut 30:12–14). The point Paul was trying to make is that not even Moses insisted that the law could make a person righteous, but rather only faith in God. Paul gave us the idea, as he had before, that the Jews were in fact given the message of redemption that was finally culminating in Christ—and many were rejecting it.

Paul said a person must "declare with your mouth" while "calling on the name of the Lord to be saved." I want to make a few points that might help us understand what Paul was trying to say:

1. *The whole point of chapters 9–11 is to reveal the Jews' need to turn to Christ.* Paul's statements are not formulaic, but rather a screenshot of what they need to do similar to what we do all the time: "Have you been baptized in Christ?" or "Have you surrendered your life to the Lord?" or "Are you a Christian?" These are all simply statements that have much more meat than the unwritten or unsaid statement that is typically understood as implied. The question that should be asked is, *What do these statements mean?*

2. *By the same token, Paul was writing to Christians.* The fact is, when you speak to Christians, you don't always have to detail every

step. If I knew you were a Christian, when I talk
to you about salvation, I could use a simple
phrase such as, "a born-again believer," and you
would know that believing, confessing,
repenting, and being baptized are implied.

3. *Furthermore, in the context of the letter, Paul
   already addressed the whole salvation plan from
   chapters 1–6.* It would be unnecessary and a
   waste of Paul's time and efforts to list everything
   again just three chapters later. At this point in
   the letter, the church knew clearly what was
   required to be in Christ.

4. *Some statements are packed with more substance
   than they seem at first glance because they have
   lost their impact over time.* For the early church
   to hear the phrase, "Calling on the name of the
   Lord," it meant something that was clear and
   known to them.

5. *Finally, we must realize the point Paul was trying
   to get across:* The Jew and Gentile alike need to
   come to salvation the same way. Paul made that
   way plain to them—They must turn to Jesus
   Christ by confessing his name and calling on
   Him. How is that done? Paul would tell you to
   re-read the first six chapters.

6. *Point: Salvation comes by Jesus Christ.*

Before we move to the next passage, I want to take a
closer look at the idea of *calling on the name of the Lord* and
how it appears in Scripture. Joel 2:28–32 is a passage quoted
by both Peter (Acts 2:21) and Paul (Rom 10:13) when they
urge their readers to "call on the name of the Lord to be

saved." This passage can easily be misused, but we are going to look at a few verses to see what this phrase means. In Acts 9:14, we read that Saul was sent to arrest all who called on the name of the Lord. The beautiful irony is that Saul, who would become Paul, would later call on the name of the Lord himself (Acts 22:16). Paul, writing to the church in Corinth, wrote;

> To the church of God in Corinth, to those sanctified in Christ Jesus and called to be His holy people, together with all those everywhere who call on the name of our Lord Jesus Christ—their Lord and ours (1 Cor 1:2).

Paul wrote to Timothy saying,

> Flee the evil desires of youth and pursue righteousness, faith, love and peace, along with those who call on the Lord... (1 Tim 2:22).

Finally, Peter wrote to the early Christians,

> Since you call on a Father who judges each person's work impartially, live out your time as foreigners here in reverent fear (1 Pet 1:17).

We come back to the question at hand; *what does it mean to call on the name of the Lord?* The phrase literally means *to invoke.* Another way of saying, *to get one's attention,* or *to compel one to act.* This is a basic concept and should be easy to understand; we invoke, appeal to, or try to get people's attention all the time. Sometimes we try a verbal appeal. However, if you were a student in school, a verbal appeal would not be as appropriate as a raising of a hand. If you were Esther, you would be ever mindful of the appropriate way to appeal to the king of Persia. If you were Ruth, you would lie at the feet of Boaz and wait for his response.

The same has been true for our approach to God. In the Old Testament, we have seen many build altars to appeal to God, to get His attention. We turn to the prophetic book of Joel where he says to *Call on the name of the Lord to be saved.* What the prophet was saying is that if people want to find salvation, they have to invoke God; they must get His attention. By invoking God, the promise was that He would respond in salvation. How do we invoke God to respond in salvation? Paul laid it out simply, and we also see Paul doing the same thing when he became a Christian. Those who run to God by believing in and proclaiming Jesus as their savior and confessing His name, repenting of their sins, and being baptized in water—This is calling on the name of the Lord. This, as God promised, will be their salvation. *Calling on the name of the Lord* is not a mere step in the salvation plan—it is the whole of what we do to get the attention of a God that yearns to save each and every one of us.

How, then, can they call on the one they have not believed in? And how can they believe in the one of whom they have not heard? And how can they hear without someone preaching to them? [15] And how can anyone preach unless they are sent? As it is written: "How beautiful are the feet of those who bring good news!" (Rom 10:14–15)

The turn of Paul's attention is not subtle, nor is it by accident. Paul just made an indicative statement saying that God will respond to any who call on Him. I imagine that at that moment Paul paused—right between verses 13 and 14. After a brief pause, he looked up with concern, but also knowing what needed to be said; *they won't know to call on God's name if we don't go and tell them!*

The churches in the early first centuries were not much different than those today, in that they were quick to recognize those who were not *part of the church*—non-Christians. It has passed through each of our minds countless times; there is a whole world out there living outside of Christ. We work with them, we bowl with them, we golf with them. Perhaps we are married to them. Every one of us knows someone who is not a Christian. The question is, *what do we do?*

Let us first face the dark and sinister truth that most of us do not like to face; if we do nothing, they likely will one day die and go to hell. What is the alternative? We could search for ways to tell them about the good news of Jesus Christ. What's the worst that could happen? What is the *best* that could happen?

"How beautiful are the feet of those who bring good news!"

But not all the Israelites accepted the good news. For Isaiah says, "Lord, who has believed our message?" Consequently, faith comes from hearing the message, and the message is heard through the word about Christ. But I ask: Did they not hear? Of course they did: "Their voice has gone out into all the earth, their words to the ends of the world." Again I ask: Did Israel not understand? First, Moses says, "I will make you envious by those who are not a nation; I will make you angry by a nation that has no understanding." And Isaiah boldly says, "I was found by those who did not seek me; I revealed myself to those who did not ask for me." But concerning Israel he says, "All day long I have held out my hands to a disobedient and obstinate people." (Rom 10:16–21)

What is the "Good News"? I think the answer is simple; it is Jesus Christ. A person might ask, *didn't they have good news already?* From what we have gathered from this chapter, the things that had unfolded in the Old Testament were designed to culminate in Jesus Christ. You could call the law *good news.* You could call the sacrifices *good news.* But as we learn from the Hebrew writer and often by Paul, these were never meant to be permanent, but were pointing toward Jesus.

Paul asked a rhetorical question; *Did they not hear?* This was an appropriate question, because if they never heard, it could be argued that they should not be held responsible. But Paul argued that the people of Israel did hear. In fact, he said that even from the days of Moses, the truth was pointing toward these days. He also used the writings of the prophet Isaiah to confirm that the message had been heard long ago. What the verses also say, however, is that so many willing ignored the message. And that is exactly what was happening.

Paul was saddened by this very point; he was writing about the Jews, his people, ones who have been devout to the ways of God from childhood. But as the promises of God were unfolding and culminating in Jesus Christ, Paul saw so many reject it all. Coming back to the first verse of this chapter, Paul said, "my heart's desire and prayer to God for the Israelites is that they may be saved."

Chapter Eleven

Paul had much anguish in his heart for his fellow Jews who have rejected Christ. Chapter eleven is the final chapter where Paul will give attention to God's desire to have both the Jews and the Gentiles as part of the kingdom. With that in mind, chapter eleven follows right behind the thoughts we saw in chapter ten; there are many Israelites who did not accept the good news of Christ. Paul began chapter eleven with a rhetorical question asking if God had rejected His people. However, the substance of the chapter is seen through an image we are given by Paul. The image is of a tree that represents the kingdom of God. We will find that God wants everyone to be grafted onto the tree. This image would also serve as an answer to the initial question; has God rejected His people? No; God desired a full tree of Gentiles *and* Jews.

> I ask then: Did God reject his people? By no means! I am an Israelite myself, a descendant of Abraham, from the tribe of Benjamin. God did not reject His people,

whom He foreknew. Don't you know what Scripture says in the passage about Elijah—how he appealed to God against Israel: "Lord, they have killed your prophets and torn down your altars; I am the only one left, and they are trying to kill me"? And what was God's answer to him? "I have reserved for myself seven thousand who have not bowed the knee to Baal." So too, at the present time there is a remnant chosen by grace. And if by grace, then it cannot be based on works; if it were, grace would no longer be grace (Rom 11:1–6).

Did God reject His people? Has there been a question as pertinent as this one? Paul spoke of God's promises and His call in Romans 9:4–5. He spoke of the foreknowledge of God in 8:29. We even have a reference to the faithfulness of God back in 3:3. The point is that Paul had been building up to this very question for a while. It was as if he was intentionally building the case and stirring their minds to already be asking the same question before they even get to this point in the letter. When the reader and listeners heard this question, they were ready and waiting for the answer—a confident *no!*

Paul brought their attention to a time in Elijah's life when he thought that all the prophets had been killed and he was the only one left. I believe one of the ideas we can take from this illustration is that God is usually doing something bigger than us. Both during the time of Paul writing this letter and during the time of Elijah, the confusion existed only while they remained ignorant of the full plan of God. For Elijah, he had to realize that God had reserved a remnant—*Elijah, you didn't see the whole picture; I am doing something big.* I believe it was the same with those during the time of Paul; God was doing something bigger than they could even imagine.

In both stories, the perception is that God had killed, or rejected, a whole group of people. But the promise of God in both stories was that He had kept a remnant of those who were faithful—not to Judaism, but to the plan of God. Paul made it clear that this remnant was not because of their good works, but only by the grace of God. A remnant is also proof that God had not rejected the Jews. The Jews had the same access as anyone else did—through grace, not by works. Furthermore, verse 16 is not really clear, but it seems that not only does God desire a remnant, but also a hope that the remnant would lead the way for the rest to come to salvation. However, not many Jews were on board with this new ideology. But what it did reveal for us is the desire for God to save all!

> What then? What the people of Israel sought so earnestly they did not obtain. The elect among them did, but the others were hardened, as it is written: "God gave them a spirit of stupor, eyes that could not see and ears that could not hear, to this very day." And David says: "May their table become a snare and a trap, a stumbling block and a retribution for them. May their eyes be darkened so they cannot see, and their backs be bent forever." (Rom 11:7–10)

They could not obtain because they pursued it as something that could be earned through their works. We need to also look at this idea of hardened hearts. Scriptures that would be useful are 2 Cor 3:14; 4:4; 2 Thess 2:8–12; and Rom 1:24–32. It is important to remember that God will never force people against their own will. When we consider those whose hearts were hardened, we are speaking of those who *already* set their feet in a direction of their own choosing. God then uses that for His glory as He focuses on the bigger picture. Notice the phrase in verse 10 where Paul spoke of their backs being bent forever. If you stop with this verse, you might be left with the idea that God did in fact reject the Jews, never to return again. However, Paul used this passage to show us that God has kept His hand reached out to receive each Jew that would come to Him—not by their works, but by grace.

> Again I ask: Did they stumble so as to fall beyond recovery? Not at all! Rather, because of their transgression, salvation has come to the Gentiles to make Israel envious. But if their transgression means riches for the world, and their loss means riches for the Gentiles, how much greater riches will their full inclusion bring! I am talking to you Gentiles. Inasmuch as I am the apostle to the Gentiles, I take pride in my ministry in the hope that I may somehow arouse my own people to envy and save some of them. For if their rejection brought reconciliation to the world, what will their acceptance be but life from the dead? If the part of the dough offered as firstfruits is holy, then the whole batch is holy; if the root is holy, so are the branches (Rom 11:11–16).

Paul's rationale through this passage was rather peculiar, but it made perfect sense in a *Paul-like way*. I am going to try to walk you through step by step: the Jewish idea was that the promise was *only* for them. However, the plan of God was different than the Jews' traditional thoughts. The Jews resisted and hardened their hearts to the fulfillment of God's plan. God's plan, in response to this, was to turn and offer salvation to the Gentiles. This action of God was intended to make the Jews envious and jealous. The big picture was clear; God wanted *all* to come to salvation.

It is also important to remember what we learned from chapter five; the plan of God is linear and was completely thought out by God before the foundation of the world. The outcome seems clear to me; God has *always* intended to save the whole world. Paul will further explain this phenomenon through the illustration of a tree in the following passage.

> If some of the branches have been broken off, and you, though a wild olive shoot, have been grafted in among the others and now share in the nourishing sap from the olive root, do not consider yourself to be superior to those other branches. If you do, consider this: You do not support the root, but the root supports you. You will say then, "Branches were broken off so that I could be grafted in." Granted. But they were broken off because of unbelief, and you stand by faith. Do not be arrogant, but tremble. For if God did not spare the natural branches, He will not spare you either (Rom 11:17–21).

Syracuse University Professor Sam Van Aken is known to have created a tree called the Tree of 40 Fruit. Each year, between the months of July and October, a variety of forty fruits ripen on this one tree. This phenomenon is explained by the technique of *grafting*, the technique used to join two or more plants or trees. This is the same idea we see here in this passage. Paul will use this idea of grafting to further prove that God did not reject His people, the Jews.

I want you to notice firstly, whose tree it is that we are reading about in the above passage? It is the kingdom of God that consisted of the Jews. God could have completely destroyed the tree and started over; after all, that was likely the thought of many. But God did not destroy it, but simply cut some branches off; He groomed the tree. Now the amazing thing is that we see God, through His grace and mercy, allowing believing Gentiles to be grafted onto this Jewish tree. This tree which represented the kingdom of God was no longer an exclusive Jewish tree, nor did it become exclusively Gentiles. It became inclusively any who would turn to Jesus in faith.

What was the purpose of Paul using this tree as an illustration? He wanted to prove two basic points: First, he wanted to prove that God did not reject the Jews. Second, we see clearly the hope that the Jews who rejected the good news of Jesus will one day repent. God will be waiting to graft them in once again.

> Consider therefore the kindness and sternness of God: sternness to those who fell, but kindness to you, provided that you continue in His kindness. Otherwise, you also will be cut off. And if they do not persist in unbelief, they will be grafted in, for God is able to graft them in again. After all, if you were cut out of an olive tree that is wild by nature, and contrary to nature were grafted into a cultivated olive tree, how much more readily will these, the natural branches, be grafted into their own olive tree! (Rom 11:22–24)

This passage is in direct reflection of what was said about the grafting of the tree. The Jews who rejected the plan of

God were cut off from the tree, experiencing the sternness
and wrath of God. However, kindness was shown to the
Gentiles who believed. Paul urged the reader to *consider*
this. God is full of love, but He also is a *just* God. Salvation is
only for those who receive the grace and mercy offered
through Jesus Christ. Any who chooses to reject Him will
sadly and inevitably experience the wrath of God.

We must not miss the heart of God seen in the passage
we are looking at. God truly wanted the Jews to return and
be grafted again into the tree. But they must do it through
Christ.

> I do not want you to be ignorant of this mystery, brothers
> and sisters, so that you may not be conceited: Israel has
> experienced a hardening in part until the full number of
> the Gentiles has come in, and in this way all Israel will be
> saved. As it is written: "The deliverer will come from
> Zion; He will turn godlessness away from Jacob. And this
> is my covenant with them when I take away their sins."
> As far as the gospel is concerned, they are enemies for
> your sake; but as far as election is concerned, they are
> loved on account of the patriarchs, for God's gifts and His
> call are irrevocable. Just as you who were at one time
> disobedient to God have now received mercy as a result
> of their disobedience, so they too have now become
> disobedient in order that they too may now receive mercy
> as a result of God's mercy to you. For God has bound
> everyone over to disobedience so that He may have mercy
> on them all (Rom 11:25–32).

It is important at this point to remember the plan of God;
it was never intended for the Jews alone—it was always for

the whole world. Even during the time of the Old Testament, there were many occasions when we see foreigners join the camp of Israel. However, over the course of time, the Jews lost track of that truth and started to believe that they were special due to their works, and all others were condemned with no hope. They did have one thing right; they were special. But what they missed was that the plan of God was to save even the lost Gentiles.

As God was unfolding His plan to offer salvation to the Gentiles, it is important to notice that the Jews still had full access as anyone else did. This was what Paul spoke of as God's gifts being *irrevocable*. All the promises were still theirs, but rather than attempting to earn them through their works, God required obedient faith. One might ask why God changed it. The truth is that it was never designed to be by works. Faith was the avenue to righteousness even from the time of Abraham. The simple answer is that the Jews had created an imbalance of faith and works to the point of not even being able to accept a savior if not based on their works.

The law had become to the Jews a list of rules they must obey to become holy. In previous verses (3:20; 5:20), Paul reminded them that the law was intended only to *reveal* sin in order to show them the need for a savior. God wanted the Jews to accept Christ and receive salvation as the rest of the world. Until then, they would be lost and rejected.

Oh, the depth of the riches of the wisdom and knowledge of God! How unsearchable His judgments, and His paths beyond tracing out! "Who has known the mind of the Lord? Or who has been His counselor?" "Who has ever given to God, that God should repay them?" For from

Him and through Him and for Him are all things. To Him be the glory forever! Amen (Rom 11:33–36).

In order to understand what just happened, we have to take note of what Paul had just finished saying. In the previous verses, Paul had been illuminating the saving mercy of God, not only for the Jews but for the whole world. That is big! That is a reason to praise God! And that is exactly what is happening in these verses; Paul began to praise God for being such a merciful God showing His love to the whole world. Paul found the intricate plan of God as something praiseworthy. Furthermore, Paul saw himself as a recipient of this plan of God's grace. And for that, he praised God.

What I find interesting is that Romans was originally written as a letter to the church in Rome. I am trying to place myself in Paul's shoes as he was writing this. There was that moment when Paul was literally writing about the mercy and saving grace of God; while doing so, these thoughts of praise flooded his mind. So, what did he do? He wrote them on the parchment as well. Using a couple of Old Testament passages to frame his thoughts, Paul put his praise on paper.

If this doxology teaches us anything, we should see that God was doing something bigger and unimaginable. For Paul, this was worthy of praise.

Chapter Twelve

We come to a change in Paul's tone of voice once again. When chapter nine began, Paul's voice became saddened and focused on his fellow Jews who rejected the gospel. Paul remained on this point from chapters 9–11. But the tone now changes. Paul was no longer focused on works of the law or righteousness. He was no longer focused on the Jew and Gentile. Now he is going to direct all his attention to general Christian living.

In several of Paul's letters, it seems that he had to address something that was to the point. In this case, Paul addresses salvation and the inclusion of the Gentiles. In each case, after Paul addressed the point, he wrote of things that were on his mind. It is possible that he had been wanting to get to this topic from the beginning of the letter, but he had to get a few important thoughts out of the way. Now that the topics of works, righteousness, Gentiles, and Jews have been exhausted, he gets to the meat of the letter; in this case, living lives of worship unto the Lord.

Notice in 1 Corinthians 3:1–4, Paul told them they were

immature and not ready for any meat, only milk. There are many reproofs and corrections in the first letter to the Corinthian believers. It is likely Paul never really got to write anything he really wanted, rather he was on defense the entire letter. Perhaps that was the purpose of the second letter. Here in the book of Romans, as we get to this portion of the letter, the church in Rome was fortunate enough for Paul to write a few things from his heart that would become treasures for us even today.

> Therefore, I urge you, brothers and sisters, in view of God's mercy, to offer your bodies as a living sacrifice, holy and pleasing to God—this is your true and proper worship. Do not conform to the pattern of this world, but be transformed by the renewing of your mind. Then you will be able to test and approve what God's will is—His good, pleasing and perfect will (Rom 12:1–2).

I want to keep this response simple and save the in-depth answer for a future study; for this time, we must be mindful that Paul was not speaking of a "time of worship," such as Sunday mornings. Paul was speaking of their daily conduct as Christians. Furthermore, the word here is better translated as "service." The subject at hand is one's daily conduct and service to God. This *service* is going to be detailed in the following verses. However, and also for a later study, these two words can be used interchangeably as they both speak of focus and reverence toward God from us.

On what grounds did Paul ask this, and why? Whenever a passage opens with a *therefore,* it is important to read the verses prior; these verses spoken of are Romans 11:33–36, where Paul wrote a doxology toward God. If you remove the chapter break, Paul simply continued to write in response to the glory of God, "Therefore..., *this is what we should be giving back to Him.*"

Paul gave us a second reason why it is becoming that we should serve the Lord in holiness—*in view of His mercies.* The mercies of God had been clearly laid out in the letter to this point. We have clearly seen that the whole plan of salvation was built on the mercy of God. For this amazing mercy bestowed upon all people, Paul found it to be the believers' reasonable response to offer themselves to God.

Paul brought us yet a third reason—*it is pleasing to God.* Simply put, if people need more reason than this, they already have missed the point.

Paul spoke of not becoming conformed to the pattern of the world. This would truly be the first form of reasonable service to God—not living according to the world's pattern but allowing God to transform us. It is important to notice the different patterns. We see different patterns all throughout life; different lifestyles, different worship styles, different clothing preferences, and so on. We also see patterns in Scripture. The Proverbs speak of patterns of the foolish and the better patterns of the wise. I presume that most of us, if not all, understand that the world also has patterns of behavior, speech, and more that are not in line with the design of God. The pattern God wants us to live is having a transformed mind. Paul said that this is our *reasonable service* to God because of all that He has done and simply for who He is. In the following verses, Paul is going to show us more of what it looks like when we allow God to transform our hearts.

For by the grace given me I say to every one of you: Do
not think of yourself more highly than you ought, but
rather think of yourself with sober judgment, in accordance with the faith God has distributed to each of you.
For just as each of us has one body with many members,
and these members do not all have the same function, so
in Christ we, though many, form one body, and each
member belongs to all the others. We have different gifts,
according to the grace given to each of us. If your gift is
prophesying, then prophesy in accordance with
your faith; if it is serving, then serve; if it is teaching, then
teach; if it is to encourage, then give encouragement; if it
is giving, then give generously; if it is to lead, do it dili-
gently; if it is to show mercy, do it cheerfully (Rom
12:3–8).

This is where Paul really began to spend time showing
the reader what it meant to live a life of service/worship unto
the Lord. The idea Paul mentioned was a *togetherness*, or a
team effort if you will. Paul wanted to remind them that they
all belonged to Christ, but also to one another. This would
have been especially important for the Jews and Gentiles to
read when regarding one another. I wonder what implica-
tions this might have when we bring it home today.

Paul did what Paul has been was known to do in his
letters; he gave us a list. The following list was what Paul
said it should look like when a person lives a life of worship
unto the Lord. I want to clarify that a person may not have
each of these completely worked out; perhaps you only have
one or two. The point is that as you live a life of worship, the
Lord is able to begin transforming you; the list below is what
Paul suggested that transformation would look like over time.

As you read this list, I want you to take note of the similarities to Galatians 5:22–23 and Colossians 3:12–14. With these lists, Paul was wanting to show the reader what Christian behavior should look like. These lists are the character and nature that God wants to work into the heart of each believer as he or she allows God to work. One might call it *Christian maturity*. Consider this list from Romans:

- Sincere love
- Hate what is evil
- Cling to what is good
- Devoted to one another
- Be zealous with spiritual fervency
- Serve the Lord
- Be joyful in hope
- Be patient in affliction
- Be faithful in prayer
- Share with the Lord's people who are in need
- Practice hospitality
- Bless those who persecute you
- Rejoice with those who rejoice
- Mourn with those who mourn
- Live in harmony with each other
- Do not be proud
- Be willing to associate with people of low position
- Do not be conceited

God truly wants His children to live the best lives possible. If you take a close look at sin, it always has one common theme—sin harms and destroys, and only offers temporary pleasures in return. However, this character God wants to

develop in us is God's way of guiding us to have the best and
most rewarding life. I challenge you to take the time to
consider each of the items listed above. First, ask if you are
developed or underdeveloped in each. If you lack in any, ask
yourself how it would change your life if you allowed God to
transform that part of you too. What will happen? There is
only one way to find out...

> Do not repay anyone evil for evil. Be careful to do what is
> right in the eyes of everyone. If it is possible, as far as it
> depends on you, live at peace with everyone. Do not take
> revenge, my dear friends, but leave room for God's wrath,
> for it is written: "It is mine to avenge; I will repay," says
> the Lord. On the contrary:"If your enemy is hungry, feed
> him; if he is thirsty, give him something to drink. In doing
> this, you will heap burning coals on his head." Do not be
> overcome by evil, but overcome evil with good (Rom
> 12:17–21).

Paul seemed to put a special emphasis on this subject;
Paul knew all too well the idea of doing evil toward others—
even if it were done with good intentions. And when Paul
became a Christian, he became the persecuted; he spoke of
some of the evils done toward him in 1 Corinthians 11:22–
33. Christians were accustomed to suffering in some ways
that are unheard of today. Jesus was crucified. Stephen was
stoned to death. All of the apostles, with the exception of
John, faced the death of a martyr. Christians were persecuted, some to death, by men like Saul of Tarsus. After Saul,
who became known as Paul, became a Christian, he would
face his own martyrdom in Rome for the name of Christ.
The fascinating thing is, in reading letters of Paul carefully,

you get the idea that Paul was aware that he might face such a demise; it did not stop him. Now we come to this passage where Paul did not question the evil inflicted upon Christians but addresses how Christians should respond to such evil.

I want you to notice from the passage that Paul did not say to just let the evil people do their worst. What he did say is to *not* let your actions be deemed evil. The fact is that sometimes a response is necessary. That is the first standard to guide our response to those who do evil. Secondly, Paul said to let our actions be found *right* in the eyes of others. Paul was trying to help us avoid personal vendettas. This means it might even be wise to talk to others for insight before you act. But at the end of the day, what you decide to do must be seen as the *right* thing to do. A third standard to guide us when responding to those who do evil to us is to remember that the goal is *peace*. This avoids any notion of payback. We also have to remember that peace can take many different forms and be achieved in different ways. But the motive of our actions must be peace. Lastly, we have to remember that if the one who does evil truly must be punished for justice to prevail, it is not our job to do so. God will make all things right, either now or when the trump sounds; He is a God of justice.

I want to take a moment to talk about this idea of *heaping coals*. I will camp out on this thought for a moment, but I believe it will be rewarding. Many have made attempts to unveil the mystery of Romans 12:20; I am hoping to shed some light on this complicated text. Paul wrote, "On the contrary: 'If your enemy is hungry, feed him; if he is thirsty, give him something to drink. In doing this, you will heap burning coals on his head.'" Some readers may have difficulty with this statement because it sounds spiteful, but the context, as we will see, suggests an alternative meaning. I will hand it to you, it is difficult to understand "heaping coals on the head of your enemy" to be a kind gesture. We will carefully look both at what Paul was trying to say and at the proverb he was citing.

There are primarily three interpretations of the end of Romans twelve, which we will discuss in just a moment, but they all come to the same conclusion. Paul wrote a few paragraphs concerning love in action, particularly toward one's enemies (Rom 12:9–21). To understand verse 20, we must keep in mind the constructive and uplifting approach Paul used. To this point, some have suggested that this verse speaks of actions that aim toward harmony with one another, and as a friend to sinners, we are to work actively in the best interest of the other. In this passage, Paul advised his readers to "bless those who persecute you" (v. 14); "do not repay anyone evil for evil" (v. 17); to "not take revenge" (v. 19); and "do not be overcome by evil, but overcome evil with good" (v. 21). With all this being said, I suggest that Paul's instructions aim not at spite but at love. It is important to keep this in mind as we look at the following interpretations.

The first interpretation of Romans 12:20—and the one I favor least—is that Christians should reserve vengeance for God. In other words, Paul was telling his readers to leave the fate of their enemies in the hands of God. Similarly, when David prayed, "May burning coals fall on them; may they be thrown into the fire, into miry pits, never to rise" (Ps 140:10), he was leaving his enemies in the hands of God just as he did in previous times with Saul (1 Sam 24; 26). This interpretation fits some of the language of Romans twelve, where we are to pay attention to our own actions while loving others and leaving judgment to God. But Romans twelve is not speaking of a passive action of letting God do something. I believe the desire of Paul was not merely to leave one's enemies in the hands of God and His vengeance, but to seek their best interest in action.

The second view is not often encountered today. In many cultures still today, people transport items on their heads, whether a bucket of water or some food or other items. In antiquity, someone might even carry on the head a pot with hot coals for the fire. At that time, the only means to heat and cook in the home was the use of fire or burning coals. Someone who ran out of hot coals might come to your home and ask for some. A loving Christian would heap those hot coals in the pot on his head. In essence, the Christian would provide even an enemy with what he needs simply because it is the good thing to do. This interpretation does reflect the unconditional love Paul was advocating, but I believe a third option gives us the fullest view of Paul's heart.

The best interpretation of this passage gives careful consideration to the context in Romans and the verses Paul cited: "If your enemy is hungry, give him food to eat; if he is thirsty, give him water to drink. In doing this, you will heap burning coals on his head, and the Lord will reward you" (Prov 25:21–22). What does this proverb mean? Consider the previous verse of Proverbs 25; "Like one who takes away a garment on a cold day, or like vinegar poured on a wound, is one who sings songs to a heavy heart" (Prov 25:20). The text is speaking of a natural uneasiness brought to enemies while doing good and the emotional discomfort they may feel when made aware of their evil conduct. Instead of retaliating, we should act in love toward our enemy and surrender him to God and his own conscience. But not to his demise;

you surrender him to his conscience and to God for the sake of peace and harmony. I am reminded of Romans 5:10 when Paul spoke of the harmony and peace which God desired with us when sending Jesus. God's love has been extended to humanity even while each and every one of us was a sinner—an enemy. We are to love our enemies and treat them kindly as God loved us and treated us kindly. The reasoning Paul suggested was that the enemy would burn with shame for his abuse of one who loves him. But to what end? To what end do we desire to heap coals upon the head of our enemy and hope his conscience is pricked? Is it just for us to be at peace with him? Romans 2:4 reminds us that "God's kindness is intended to lead you to repentance." We know from 2 Peter 3:9 that God desires everyone to repent. Our actions, whatever they may be, must be to lead a person to this same end.

A careful reading of Romans 12:9–21 will show that Paul was urging the people to love actively and pray for their enemies; no sort of evil intent toward one's enemy is warranted. We do have enemies who may need punishment, but that fact ought not to change our behavior nor is their punishment to be our concern. We are to leave any injustices to God and seek to be at peace with our enemies as much as it is in our power; we are to strive to give to our enemies what is in their best interest. Paul was speaking of a selfless love to those who do not deserve it but need it. Paul was speaking about an active love that, if administered, will change lives. Paul was speaking of the love of God being displayed through us toward our enemies as it was first displayed through God to us.

Paul wanted each member of the church in Rome to be an overcomer. He made a big deal about this when painting the victorious picture of a Christian as an *overcomer* in

Christ (Rom 8:37). Paul wanted to see the church in Rome follow hard after God and walk in faith, not by works, and not let their differences separate them. For us today, this journey of living as an overcomer begins with submitting ourselves to the Lord as a living sacrifice. This is when transformation takes place and we become molded into the character of God. This is when lives are changed around us. Do you want to overcome evil? Through Christ, let goodness prevail in your own life first.

Chapter Thirteen

When studying the Bible, you realize that some chapter breaks should not be there. After all, they were placed there many years later to help readers like us navigate through the pages. The editors tried to place the chapter breaks in appropriate places, but sometimes, they oddly placed the chapter break in mid-thought. That is what we have here as we journey into chapter thirteen.

At the beginning of chapter twelve, Paul began to discuss matters of Christian behavior; what Paul called *a life of worship*. Paul wrote that it was a person's *reasonable service*. Paul spoke of a person's humble service as part of the whole body of Christ. Paul also gave very explicit characteristics in a list form. But when we came to the end of chapter twelve, Paul was not finished. Chapter thirteen carries on the same thought of what it means to be a Christian living a life of worship unto the Lord.

Let everyone be subject to the governing authorities, for there is no authority except that which God has established. The authorities that exist have been established by God. Consequently, whoever rebels against the authority is rebelling against what God has instituted, and those who do so will bring judgment on themselves. For rulers hold no terror for those who do right, but for those who do wrong. Do you want to be free from fear of the one in authority? Then do what is right and you will be commended. For the one in authority is God's servant for your good. But if you do wrong, be afraid, for rulers do not bear the sword for no reason. They are God's servants, agents of wrath to bring punishment on the wrongdoer. Therefore, it is necessary to submit to the authorities, not only because of possible punishment but also as a matter of conscience. This is also why you pay taxes, for the authorities are God's servants, who give their full time to governing. Give to everyone what you owe them: If you owe taxes, pay taxes; if revenue, then revenue; if respect, then respect; if honor, then honor (Rom 13:1–7).

Before we begin to dig into the detail of this passage, I want to preface something important; this passage was not intended by Paul nor by me to show any approval or disapproval of any particular political party. I believe this passage is not complicated; it only becomes so when people manipulate it for selfish reasons. For Paul to write this passage for us speaks volumes for us even today and how we respond to governments. There have been times when the tension rises during election times. Let's face it, no one is happy to see *the other guy* elected that you did not vote for. Furthermore, what do you do when you feel the political power is corrupt? What do we do as Christians? Paul would say that the political party and its moral standing should have no bearing on how Christians should act. When Paul wrote this passage, the ruling government was not Christian, nor was it even his people; Israel was overrun and ruled by a foreign nation. The world, including Jerusalem and all of Israel (the promised land), was overthrown by the Roman Empire some one-hundred years prior. It was during this same Roman subjection that Jesus told His disciples to pay taxes as the government required. It was the same Roman government that gave permission to crucify Jesus. A few years after Paul would write this letter, he would travel to Rome and there would suffer the death of a martyr. Only about five years after the death of Paul, the Roman government would march on Jerusalem and destroy it, leaving no stone unturned. This was the context in which Paul wrote, *be subjected to your governing authorities.* And that brings us to one last thing to consider; the church in Rome was right in the middle of this pagan power and would feel the heat of its ruthless leadership more than any other. For many, these words would have been hard to swallow. But for Paul, it was what it took to be a true Christian living a life of worship to God.

The first item written by Paul was to be subjected to the governing authorities. The word *subject* means exactly what many would suspect: to submit under one's authority, leadership, respect, and taxes included. This can be a very difficult place. Let's face it, it is easy to subject yourself under the authority of a government that is righteous and makes good rules, but how often has that been the case since Saul became king in First Samuel 9 and 10? The true test of character is when we subject to such authority not because of their morality, but because of our character.

Paul continued to say that *every* governing authority is established by God. This does not mean that God approves of the lifestyle or actions of every ruler; consider Isaiah 44:28 and 45:1:

Who says of Cyrus, "He is my shepherd and will accomplish all that I please; he will say of Jerusalem, 'Let it be rebuilt,' and of the temple, 'Let its foundations be laid.'"

and

This is what the Lord says to his anointed, to Cyrus, whose right hand I take hold of to subdue nations before him and to strip kings of their armor, to open doors before him so that gates will not be shut.

In these two verses, Isaiah spoke of Cyrus. Cyrus was not a godly king by any measure, yet he was called "God's anointed." God had placed Cyrus on the throne for a purpose; a purpose bigger than that of Cyrus. Many times in history, God had placed His people under an evil ruler. A closer look at each of these stories would reveal that God was developing and maturing His people. The key in this passage is that God is in control—moreover, God was doing something bigger than we usually can see. There are several stories in Scripture that reveal the same pattern. In each, we realize that God is always at work in and amongst His people. However, this is most often seen best in hindsight.

For rulers hold no terror for those who do right, but for those who do wrong. A person can quickly respond with many examples of a government holding terror over its people. I do not propose to have all the answers, but I will give you my best view of this Scripture. The purpose of government is order. And if we look at history, we will realize that the church has always been provided *more* freedom than if there was no government order. Furthermore, rarely in history have there been cases when the government was hunting down and killing Christians. I did not say never, but rarely. Consider the destruction of Jerusalem in 70 AD. Many historians speak of Jewish revolts that led to Roman retaliation. We see many cases of martyrdom in the Bible and in the early centuries. A good number of these were not from government persecution, but rather religious animosity most often coming from the Jews; a perfect example would be the death of Christ. Also, notice Paul's situation when he was in jail in Jerusalem and Caesarea (Acts 23–26). The Roman authorities did not know what to do with Paul, nor did they really care. Again, as it was with Christ, the situation was heated and fueled by the Jews. I know that government policies and acceptance of Christianity vary around the world. I know that in some places, there is some persecution from governing authorities. However, I believe historically, governing authorities have done more *good* than *harm* to Christians, and have provided more freedom than if there was no order.

Now we have to address the topic no one likes, but we are taunted by it every day—taxes. You can't even make a purchase or sale without the government trying to take its cut. Samuel tried to warn the people of Israel about the repercussions of having a king; taxes is one of them (1 Sam 8). The people disregarded the advice of Samuel and insisted on a king. From that day forward, people have been complaining about taxes. Jesus also was asked about taxes. The people thought, *now that the Messiah is here, maybe we can get out from under the bondage of taxes.* Jesus's answer was clear and concise; give unto Caesar what is Caesar's (Matt 22:21; Mark 12:17)—pay taxes! This is exactly what Paul told them to do as well. And remember, the government during the time of Paul was as wicked as they get. So, paying taxes is not a matter of the government's morality and therefore deserving of your subjecting. Paying taxes is a matter of one's good conscience to God, knowing that your government, evil or good, has been established by God. This can be a lot to chew on, but Paul did not beat around the bush; this is what a life of worship should look like for the Christian.

I think there is a big-picture element that has to be considered here; God is very concerned about developing men and women who know authority and respect. I believe this is for a couple of reasons. Firstly, it often provides the best social outcome in just about any culture: children respecting their parents; children respecting their teachers in school; husbands and wives respecting one another; the public respecting police officers; citizens respecting laws; congregations respecting church leadership. I can go on, but the point is made. And I believe a person of respect is just that—a person of respect. Therefore, if parents train their children to be respectful at home, they will likely be respectful at school. They will likely respect the officer if they get pulled over one day, and so on. Respect is rooted in one's own character.

The second reason I believe God wants to develop men and women who know authority and respect is that that same respect is due back to God. Some might call it the fear of the Lord. It is this attitude toward God and His word that will guide a person in living a life of worship. When a person can sit before the Lord and say, *God, I am listening*, that is respect—life-changing respect. But here it is; if people don't have that respect in their day-to-day with parents, with officers, with the government, or with church eldership, they likely will not have it with God. I come back to the simple statement I made above; A person of respect is *a person of respect*. That respect will permeate every area of one's life. When we mature this respect in our day-to-day interactions with others, things will be well for us. When we grow in this respect toward God, that is the beginning of the amazing life-changing journey of living a life of worship to God.

> Let no debt remain outstanding, except the continuing debt to love one another, for whoever loves others has fulfilled the law. The commandments, "You shall not commit adultery," "You shall not murder," "You shall not steal," "You shall not covet," and whatever other command there may be, are summed up in this one command: "Love your neighbor as yourself." Love does no harm to a neighbor. Therefore love is the fulfillment of the law (Rom 13:8–10).

> If I speak in the tongues[a] of men or of angels, but do not have love, I am only a resounding gong or a clanging cymbal. If I have the gift of prophecy and can fathom all mysteries and all knowledge, and if I have a faith that can move mountains, but do not have love, I am nothing. If I give all I possess to the poor and give over my body to hardship that I may boast, but do not have love, I gain

nothing. Love is patient, love is kind. It does not envy, it does not boast, it is not proud. It does not dishonor others, it is not self-seeking, it is not easily angered, it keeps no record of wrongs. Love does not delight in evil but rejoices with the truth. It always protects, always trusts, always hopes, always perseveres. Love never fails. But where there are prophecies, they will cease; where there are tongues, they will be stilled; where there is knowledge, it will pass away. For we know in part and we prophesy in part, but when completeness comes, what is in part disappears. When I was a child, I talked like a child, I thought like a child, I reasoned like a child. When I became a man, I put the ways of childhood behind me. For now we see only a reflection as in a mirror; then we shall see face to face. Now I know in part; then I shall know fully, even as I am fully known. And now these three remain: faith, hope and love. But the greatest of these is love. (1 Cor 13)

Where else would Paul climax a life of worship than in the greatest command? In his writing, Paul enjoyed his *play on words*. He did the same thing in Ephesians 5:18 when he mentioned drunkenness; you realize that Paul was not addressing drunkenness at all, but rather a full submission to the Holy Spirit. Likewise, the topic here is not debt, as in financial; Paul was talking about love. Yes, the implication is that a person should not have debt, but if that is all a person gets out of this passage, he missed the main thing. The emphasis suggests that *if* you owe anything to a person, let it be your love. This is not only the greatest command, but Paul believed it to be the very core of living a life of worship unto God.

It is important to notice that Paul was careful not to imply a disregard for the law. Rather, he showed how it could be fully satisfied and accomplished in a person's life—through love. The same message is seen in Paul's letter to the church in Corinth: and was also the conclusion Jesus came to as we see in Matthew 22:35–40 and Mark 12:28–34. There is no law left undone when a person practices love.

> One of them, an expert in the law, tested him with this question: "Teacher, which is the greatest commandment in the Law?" Jesus replied: "'Love the Lord your God with all your heart and with all your soul and with all your mind.' This is the first and greatest commandment. And the second is like it: 'Love your neighbor as yourself.' All the Law and the Prophets hang on these two commandments" (Matt 22:35–40).

> One of the teachers of the law came and heard them debating. Noticing that Jesus had given them a good answer, he asked him, "Of all the commandments, which is the most important?" "The most important one," answered Jesus, "is this: 'Hear, O Israel: The Lord our God, the Lord is one. Love the Lord your God with all your heart and with all your soul and with all your mind and with all your strength.' The second is this: 'Love your neighbor as yourself.' There is no commandment greater than these." "Well said, teacher," the man replied. "You are right in saying that God is one and there is no other but Him. To love Him with all your heart, with all your understanding and with all your

strength, and to love your neighbor as yourself is more important than all burnt offerings and sacrifices." When Jesus saw that he had answered wisely, He said to him, "You are not far from the kingdom of God." And from then on no one dared ask Him any more questions (Mark 12:28–34).

And do this, understanding the present time: The hour has already come for you to wake up from your slumber, because our salvation is nearer now than when we first believed. The night is nearly over; the day is almost here. So let us put aside the deeds of darkness and put on the armor of light. Let us behave decently, as in the daytime, not in carousing and drunkenness, not in sexual immorality and debauchery, not in dissension and jealousy. Rather, clothe yourselves with the Lord Jesus Christ, and do not think about how to gratify the desires of the flesh (Rom 13:11–14).

This passage is *not* speaking of the end of the world. In fact, my opinion is that none of Paul's writings in Romans imply or reference the *end of the world*. This will be referenced in more detail in another study. This passage was intended to be a wake-up call for the reader and is a timeless message that is no less relevant for us today. I don't think this passage is to imply that the church in Rome was spiritually sleeping, as was the church in Sardis (Rev 3:2). Paul's encouragement was simple; stay vigilant and awake. This was the message of the early church and is still needed today. Why do we need to stay vigilant? Because we truly do not know how much time any of us have. In many places in Scripture, they were encouraged not to worry about tomorrow, but be vigilant today (1 Cor 16:13; 2 Tim 4:5; Eph 5:15; Col 4:2; 1 Pet 5:8).

The final thought of this chapter is not exactly a high note, but it is a very important one. Paul spoke of making the most of our time and staying awake and being vigilant. Following the format of several of Paul's letters, we are given a list of sins. Paul suggested that we don't have time to live in those sins. There is too much work to be done for the kingdom. The world, which is waiting to be told the gospel, does not have time for us Christians to be living in sin. Peter wrote it this way when addressing the early Christians, "For you have spent enough time in the past doing what pagans choose to do—living in debauchery, lust, drunkenness, orgies, carousing and detestable idolatry" (1 Pet 4:3). Yes, we have; we all have spent enough time in sin. It is time to wake up, be vigilant, and live a life of worship unto God.

Chapter Fourteen

In this chapter, Paul is going to yet continue the topic of Christian living, or what he called *a life of worship unto God*. Although it did look like Paul was concluding the topic with the awesome climax of love, he was not done yet. In the past couple of chapters, Paul had been speaking to the church in Rome about a generic, yet important topic; a life of worship is an appropriate topic for any Christian. However, in this chapter, Paul is going to narrow the focus on a matter that was specifically relevant to the church in Rome. This does not mean it will not be appropriate for us today or for any other Christian; I think this topic has become no less relevant. The topic of *matters of opinion* or *debatable matters* is a topic that Paul felt the church in Rome needed to be admonished.

The church in Rome was a very diverse group; this is evident just from the early chapters of this letter. The church consisted of both Jews and Gentiles, but since the church was positioned in the center of the pagan world, it likely was much more diverse than even that. The individuals in the church in Rome, although they agreed on the *important* things, would have been diverse in many ways: religious background, ethnic heritage, moral values, holy practices, eating and drinking habits, sacrifices, celebrations, special days, and more. Paul wrote this portion of the letter to help them to be united with one another in Christ even while so different in many ways. In this letter, these differences are called disputable matters—some translations call them *matters of opinion* or also *debatable matters*.

> Accept the one whose faith is weak, without quarreling over disputable matters. One person's faith allows them to eat anything, but another, whose faith is weak, eats only vegetables. The one who eats everything must not treat with contempt the one who does not, and the one who does not eat everything must not judge the one who does, for God has accepted them. Who are you to judge someone else's servant? To their own master, servants stand or fall. And they will stand, for the Lord is able to make them stand. One person considers one day more sacred than another; another considers every day alike. Each of them should be fully convinced in their own mind. Whoever regards one day as special does so to the Lord. Whoever eats meat does so to the Lord, for they give thanks to God; and whoever abstains does so to the Lord and gives thanks to God. For none of us lives for ourselves alone, and none of us dies for ourselves alone. If we live, we live for the Lord; and if we die, we die for the Lord. So, whether we live or die, we belong to the Lord. For this very reason, Christ died and returned to life so that He might be the Lord of both the dead and the living (Rom 14:1–9).

Matters of opinion; this phrase fits my vocabulary a little better and gives the same message as *disputable matters*. Matters of opinion are those things we may not agree on, but they do not have a *right* or *wrong* value; they might just be *different*. Matters of opinion are impacted by a person's background, immediate circumstances, ethnicity, gender, economic status, etc. Each person simply looks at life differently than literally every other person and will interpret things differently. Many times, these are matters of opinion.

I am not saying the truth is subjective. We must keep in mind that the subject is not indisputable matters that are clearly right or wrong; we are talking about *matters of opinion*. We are talking about matters that do not impact one's salvation. Some of the examples Paul gave were the choice of what foods to eat and what days a person celebrates. I believe there is a *rule of thumb* a person can follow to rightly apply this principle today. Matters of opinion can be more clearly defined by the things that are *not* clearly mandated in Scripture. There are practices as Christians that we adhere to because Scripture gives a clear command. Yet, there are also practices a Christian might adopt that do not flow from a clear command, but rather seem prudent after an honest reading of Scripture; these would be more matters of opinion.

I want to clarify what Paul would *not* have thought to be a matter of opinion. There are some things in Scripture that are clearly mandated to do or not to do; these are not up for opinion, but rather a simple acceptance and obedience. Some matters I see clearly in Scripture are: Do we need Jesus for salvation? Am I permitted to have sex with a partner I am not married to? Do I need to make my best efforts to assemble for worship? Am I permitted to murder, lie, or commit adultery? Etc. These matters and more are not matters of opinion because there are clear references in Scripture that show us what God desires. However, some things are not so clear.

There are *many* matters that I believe are matters of opinion. These are items that have not been clearly addressed in Scripture; however, we still have to make a judgment call on where we stand. Because these matters are not clearly addressed in Scripture, it is often and likely that we might differ in opinion; that is the point of this chapter. And Paul was attempting to help us understand that these matters should not divide us. What are some matters of opinion? Dances; tattoos; movie theaters; working or doing anything on Sunday; what ratings of movies to allow; listening to secular music; interpretation of Revelation; versions of the Bible; special days (birthdays, holidays, etc.); and the list goes on and on. The reason I have listed these is that these are matters that are not clearly addressed in Scripture. There are some of them I would love to have a stronger opinion on, but it is important to separate and distinguish what is Scripture from what is your tradition and preference. There are some things that God simply did not give us a clear mandate, we call them matters of opinion; it is okay if we disagree. Paul continued to give direction as to *how* to disagree, yet not divide.

Paul addressed those with a weak faith. Paul was speaking about those who cannot bring themselves to break from traditions that they have walked in—the immediate context was Judaism. Paul did not tell the Jews or the Gentiles they had to change. But in these matters of opinion, they were instructed to respect one another. This would have been extremely hard for the upright Jew being told to accept the Gentile who was eating whatever he wanted while not adhering to some of the traditions the Jews were raised with. This would have also been difficult for the Gentiles looking at the Jews who were stuck in their old practices. Both would have been tempted to see the other as *wrong*. Paul's response was: *some things are just different.*

We cannot leave this section before we notice and give the following passage careful thought; read the following again:

> Whoever regards one day as special does so to the Lord. Whoever eats meat does so to the Lord, for they give thanks to God; and whoever abstains does so to the Lord and gives thanks to God. For none of us lives for ourselves alone, and none of us dies for ourselves alone. If we live, we live for the Lord; and if we die, we die for the Lord. So, whether we live or die, we belong to the Lord (Rom 14:6–8).

When I read this section, I imagine that we could put a simple modern phrase to this passage that would simplify things; "Mind your own business." The believers were all getting in each other's business, but Paul said, that is between them and God. A person might ask, what if someone is living in sin? That is entirely a different matter that both Jesus and Paul addressed; but not the subject here. Here, we are talking about *matters of opinion.* What does this mean? There are some things that are not clearly addressed in Scripture. But each of us has to make a choice on these matters. I make that choice and will stand account-able to God. God wants me to stand fully convinced of my decision and stand on it. We live and die to the Lord, and we belong only to the Lord.

> You, then, why do you judge your brother or sister? Or why do you treat them with contempt? For we will all stand before God's judgment seat. It is written: "'As surely as I live,' says the Lord, 'every knee will bow before me; every tongue will acknowledge God.'" So then, each of us will give an account of ourselves to God. Therefore let us stop passing judgment on one another. Instead, make up your mind not to put any stumbling block or obstacle in the way of a brother or sister. I am convinced, being fully persuaded in the Lord Jesus, that nothing is unclean in itself. But if anyone regards something as unclean, then for that person it is unclean. If your brother or sister is distressed because of what you eat, you are no longer acting in love. Do not by your eating destroy someone for whom Christ died. Therefore do not let what you know is good be spoken of as evil. For the kingdom of God is not a matter of eating and drinking, but of righteousness, peace and joy in the Holy Spirit, because anyone who serves Christ in this way is pleasing to God and receives human approval (Rom 14:10–18).

I think in this passage, we begin to see more clearly what Paul's point was. We see him say the same thing back in verses 3 and 4, and we are brought back to it now. The point Paul was trying to make is that the church was not intended to be judgmental—neither towards one another nor outsiders. Notice the religious world during the time of Jesus and Paul; the ones who thought themselves to be the most righteous were also those who looked down on all others who were not like them—the Pharisees and Sadducees. However, when we see the church established by Christ and during the days of Paul, there was no advocacy for judgment, rather Christians were encouraged to look inward. The church in Rome had some of those Jewish converts as part of their membership. Remember, the Jews were entrusted the Word of God; they would likely have known the Old Testament Scriptures and holy living more aptly than the Gentiles. But Paul did not want them to use this to become prideful and stir divisions. Paul wanted them to stay far away from looking down on one another because of differences. Paul wanted them to know that there are some things that are matters of opinion, and one day each of us will be held accountable for those things only before God. But before one another, we owe respect and love.

What if our freedom becomes a stumbling block to another person? For example, what if a person believes it is okay to listen to secular music, but a Christian friend of theirs thinks it is a sin? Using this passage to guide us, it seems that Paul would suggest turning the music off while inviting those friends over. The purpose is not to be deceitful, but rather to not create a stumbling block. It is when our freedoms start becoming divisive and a stumbling block to others that we have bigger issues to deal with. Paul will address this a little more in the next section.

Let us therefore make every effort to do what leads to peace and to mutual edification. Do not destroy the work of God for the sake of food. All food is clean, but it is wrong for a person to eat anything that causes someone else to stumble. It is better not to eat meat or drink wine or to do anything else that will cause your brother or sister to fall. So whatever you believe about these things keep between yourself and God. Blessed is the one who does not condemn himself by what he approves. But whoever has doubts is condemned if they eat, because their eating is not from faith; and everything that does not come from faith is sin (Rom 14:19–23).

We have evident freedoms that come from being in Christ. However, Paul was careful to remind us that there are parameters that must be placed around how we exercise those freedoms. The first parameter Paul set was that we must seek to be at peace with others. This does not mean that we do everything to please others, but if momentarily setting aside a freedom will secure a relationship, that is the priority. Furthermore, our actions must edify others. It is so easy to get caught up in our freedoms, that we can sometimes forget that our actions are first to edify.

I want to take a moment to look at this particular phrase, "Do not destroy the work of God for the sake of food." People have always been prone to have something tangible to show the work of God in their lives. For the early church, this was the struggle with the idea of circumcision. For some, the work of God is how good they could be, or for some, making sure their church attendance is stellar. In the context of these chapters, Paul was suggesting that the work of God was not demonstrated through what we eat or drink. For Paul, the work of God was demonstrated through one's character development. Therefore, Paul was saying not to diminish the amazing work of God in the things we eat or drink; there is so much more the Lord is wanting to do in a person.

Paul said that each person must do what he believes is

right, and do it out of faith. The word faith means to be fully persuaded or convinced. Each and every one of us must decide on these matters of opinion ourselves. The criteria, or parameter, is that deep within, each of us has to be convinced that it is right to do. Paul referred to this as the law of conscience in Romans 2:15. What if a person is not convinced of something? He should not do it, for to him it is sin.

Although I titled this lesson "Matters of Opinion," it is not the primary point of Paul. Knowing how diverse the church in Rome was, Paul wanted to address these differences before they had a chance to cause harm to the church. Paul did not want the people to put up walls and barriers of division between one another over matters that God did not intend to be divisive. The same is true for us today. We must be mindful of the matters that are rooted in our own opinion rather than the Word of God. There are many things that God did not address clearly. I believe He left these matters up to His people to exercise freedom. Perhaps it is the ultimate test of love and acceptance.

Chapter Fifteen

As Paul was wrapping up this lengthy letter to the church in Rome, he gave a few final and encouraging thoughts while first tying up the previous conversation on matters of opinion. In doing so, he stressed the encouragement of the Scriptures. Again, we will see an oddly placed chapter break. This is not a big deal unless it leads a person to think the subject has changed as well. In this case, as we open up chapter fifteen, we see that Paul was still wrapping up matters of opinion. As long as we have that in mind, this should be a smooth transition. Near the latter part of this chapter, it seems evident that Paul thought this letter would reach Rome only a few weeks before he planned to. But as we will see later, things did not happen as Paul had planned. Nonetheless, Paul shared that he was very excited to have plans to go to Rome, and in fact, also go to Spain, which we have little evidence that he ever made it there. With no further ado, let's begin chapter fifteen.

We who are strong ought to bear with the failings of the weak and not to please ourselves. Each of us should please our neighbors for their good, to build them up. For even Christ did not please Himself but, as it is written: "The insults of those who insult you have fallen on me." (Rom 15:1–3)

These beginning verses are a continuation of the previous thought in chapter fourteen—matters of opinion. We all have found differences among each other. No matter how much you love people, they are simply different and unique beings. Paul was writing these verses to help the reader know what it means to take the high road. Or if we want to use the language Paul introduced in 12:1–2, live a *life of worship unto the Lord.*

When we come to tough situations where we have to choose an action and a response when dealing with other people, Paul gave two very concise responses to consider: first, our response must be *for their good.* Whether it is an argument with a co-worker, our children, or with our spouse. And regardless if the argument is about theology, how to perform duty at work, or parenting styles, Paul gave us this parameter: let your response, the tone, and the motive, be given *for their good.* Secondly, Paul said our responses must *build them up.* Again, no matter the context, the exhortation is the same. Our responses should be rooted in who we are, not who we are talking to. So, whether we are at work, talking with our spouse, or our children; is what we are saying, and how we are saying it intended to *build them up?* I urge us to take time to reflect on these two response styles and consider how this can change so much.

Paul used Psalm 69:9 to show how Jesus allowed the insults to come at Him because He had the bigger picture in mind. It is so easy to want to protect ourselves and defend ourselves from insults and ridicule. But while doing so, we often start responding in ways that do not build anyone up and are in no way for the good of the one with whom we are conversing. When we make it about ourselves, we quickly abandon these relevant principles Paul was handing us in these verses. By Paul quoting Psalm 69:9, Paul was trying to show the reader that Jesus made every action *for our good*; furthermore, His actions, from start to finish, were to *build us up*. What did that look like? He allowed the insults. He allowed the abuse. He put Himself aside.

These verses were written with the intention to guide the members of the church in Rome when dealing with difficult matters of disagreement. If the character of a Christian cannot even guide us through peace-making with other Christians, then what do we have to offer the world? The message in these chapters is no less relevant now than it was two-thousand years ago. God still expects His people to grow in His character and put on the nature of Christ. We need to stop fighting over and for our opinions and put the other person above us. We need to stop dividing simply because someone else does not agree with us.

For everything that was written in the past was written to teach us, so that through the endurance taught in the Scriptures and the encouragement they provide we might have hope. May the God who gives endurance and encouragement give you the same attitude of mind toward each other that Christ Jesus had, so that with one mind and one voice you may glorify the God and Father of our Lord Jesus Christ. Accept one another, then, just as Christ accepted you, in order to bring praise to God. For I tell you that Christ has become a servant of the Jews on behalf of God's truth, so that the promises made to the patriarchs might be confirmed and, moreover, that the Gentiles might glorify God for his mercy. As it is written: "Therefore I will praise you among the Gentiles; I will sing the praises of your name." Again, it says, "Rejoice, you Gentiles, with his people." And again, "Praise the Lord, all you Gentiles; let all the peoples extol him." And again, Isaiah says, "The Root of Jesse will spring up, one who will arise to rule over the nations; in Him the Gentiles will hope." May the God of hope fill you with all joy and peace as you trust in Him, so that you may over-flow with hope by the power of the Holy Spirit (Rom 15:4–13).

What is *everything* referring to? Paul said, "for *everything* that was written in the past was written to teach us..." I believe the most evident answer is the Old Testament, which was referred to as Scripture during the early church. This was congruent with what Paul wrote to young Timothy, saying, "All Scripture is God-breathed and is useful for teaching, rebuking, correcting and training in righteousness" (2 Tim 3:16). There was no *New Testament* book written, or at least recognized as *Scripture* at that time yet. The *everything* that was written was the Old Testament Scriptures. This does not belittle the usefulness of the New Testament at all; However, it shows us the usefulness of the Old as well New.

Paul had a few things to say about the Old Testament Scriptures: firstly, they were useful for our teaching. Often in Paul's letters, he referred back to stories in the Old Testament to help clarify his point. In this letter alone, he often referenced Abraham and Moses, and also the Psalms. Why? because Old Testament Scripture was useful for teaching. Secondly, Paul spoke of the *endurance* taught in the Scriptures. This becomes evident when reading about Job, Moses, Joshua, David, the prophets, and so many more; we read how they endured hardship through the help of God. Paul was suggesting that these stories pay forward a relevant message to us today. Thirdly, Paul said that the Scriptures provide encouragement. When we read through the Old Testament, we see so many stories of God's mercy, His love, and His salvation. These stories were not written without purpose. They were intended to teach us about our God. As we become aware of the loving nature of God, we should be *encouraged* to be His children. Lastly, Paul said that all these things were intended to give us hope; the teaching, the endurance, the encouragement—hope. God wants us to *overflow* with hope (verse 13).

What is hope? It is an expectation; it is having something to look forward to. Paul suggested that as we look *back* into the Old Testament Scriptures, we learn such amazing things about God. We should be able to take this knowledge about God and look forward, knowing and being confident that God has never changed, and He will walk with us as He has always walked with His people—that is hope.

The next passage, verses 5–13, may seem at first to be a disconnected thought; however, I want to show you what Paul was trying to do. God had given His people endurance and encouragement. This is the very source of the hope we have in Him. Paul suggested that God wants to give us even more; God wants to give us the same attitude as Christ. That is rich! Having the same mind as Christ is for the purpose that God may be glorified through us. *Paul, where are you going with this?* Paul was coming right back to one of the underlining themes of the book—unity between God's people; the Jews and Gentiles alike.

What does it look like when there is unity, even amongst those who are different than yourself? You begin to accept one another, understanding that every person is different and unique in one way or another. We come to realize that not one of us will have the same view on *every* matter. Furthermore, and above all, we accept one another as Christ accepted us. And what Paul was showing the readers is that Christ has equally accepted *everyone*. Using several Scriptures from what we now call the Old Testament, Paul showed that God poured out His mercy not only on the Jews but also on the Gentiles. Each would have equal access to respond to the salvation plan of God through Jesus Christ.

> I myself am convinced, my brothers and sisters, that you yourselves are full of goodness, filled with knowledge and competent to instruct one another. Yet I have written you quite boldly on some points to remind you of them again, because of the grace God gave me to be a minister of Christ Jesus to the Gentiles. He gave me the priestly duty of proclaiming the gospel of God, so that the Gentiles might become an offering acceptable to God, sanctified by the Holy Spirit. Therefore I glory in Christ Jesus in my service to God. I will not venture to speak of anything

except what Christ has accomplished through me in leading the Gentiles to obey God by what I have said and done—by the power of signs and wonders, through the power of the Spirit of God. So from Jerusalem all the way around to Illyricum, I have fully proclaimed the gospel of Christ. It has always been my ambition to preach the gospel where Christ was not known, so that I would not be building on someone else's foundation. Rather, as it is written: "Those who were not told about Him will see, and those who have not heard will understand." This is why I have often been hindered from coming to you (Rom 15:14–22).

Paul was one who would write things just the way they were. You can quickly see this in his letter to the churches in Galatia, especially in his first letter to the church in Corinth. If Paul had an issue to address, he would just come out and say it. At the same time, when Paul offered a statement of praise, it was not flattery, but from the same sincerity as every word within his writings. And this is exactly how Paul began this next passage; he praised them, saying that he was convinced that what he has been writing about, they already were doing well. In essence, this letter, while offering instruction, was also an encouragement to keep on doing the good that they had been.

I want to take note of verse 18, because this underlines the whole ministry of Paul, and can be seen in each of Paul's letters —"I will not venture to speak of anything except what Christ has accomplished through me in leading the Gentiles to obey God by what I have said and done—." Paul was an apostle with a message that was meant to go beyond the borders of Jerusalem. Paul wanted to make sure the Gentiles understood that the saving power of Jesus was for them as well. And Paul was so zealous to say that he longed to go to places he had not yet visited and tell those who had never heard. Paul reasoned that this might be why he had been delayed in coming to Rome; they had already been given the gospel. However, as we will see in the next passage, Paul was making intent plans to visit this church. The plans would not go nearly as planned by any measure, but he will get there.

> But now that there is no more place for me to work in these regions, and since I have been longing for many years to visit you, I plan to do so when I go to Spain. I hope to see you while passing through and to have you assist me on my journey there, after I have enjoyed your company for a while. Now, however, I am on my way to Jerusalem in the service of the Lord's people there. For Macedonia and Achaia were pleased to make a contribution for the poor among the Lord's people in Jerusalem. They were pleased to do it, and indeed they owe it to them. For if the Gentiles have shared in the Jews' spiritual blessings, they owe it to the Jews to share with them their material blessings. So after I have completed this task and have made sure that they have received this contribution, I will go to Spain and visit you on the way. I know that when I come to you, I will come in the full measure of the blessing of Christ. I urge you, brothers and sisters, by our Lord Jesus Christ and by the love of the Spirit, to join me in my struggle by praying to God for me. Pray that I may be kept safe from the unbelievers in Judea and that the contribution I take to Jerusalem may be favorably received by the Lord's people there, so that I may come to you with joy,

by God's will, and in your company be refreshed (Rom
15:23–32).

Paul had journeyed to many places preaching the gospel.
Several of the places he had visited two or three times. He
had been preaching in the areas of Asia and Greece for about
ten years, and in Paul's assessment, he had completed the
mission and was now ready to move to another location. He
preached and taught the gospel. He pioneered churches. He
established preachers, elders, and deacons in some of the
churches. He wrote letters to instruct, edify, and build up.
But now it was time to leave. Paul explained to the church in
Rome what his plans were; he would deliver the money to
Jerusalem, then hit the road and head to Spain. On his way
to Spain, Paul would stop by Rome.

The plan would not unfold as Paul had hoped. He asked
the church in Rome to pray that all would go well for him
when he was in Jerusalem, but it did not seem to go so well
(Acts 21). Don't get me wrong, God was very much in
control, but things were not going exactly as Paul thought
they would. Paul delivered the contribution to the church,
but then there were some who plotted against him and he
was arrested. Granted, it was not a big deal for Paul to be
behind bars in a jail cell; a common scene for his ambitious
ministry. However, this time was different. Between
Jerusalem and then Caesarea, Paul would be imprisoned for
about two years, until he finally appealed to Caesar (Acts
21–26). As you continue reading in the two final chapters of
Acts, Paul, as a prisoner, was placed on a ship and sent to
Rome. After a long and extraordinary journey, the final
verses in Acts show Paul under house arrest in Rome, then
the book closes.

It seems evident that Paul was able to eventually visit the church in Rome. However, rather than a few weeks following the letter, it was a couple of years. We do not have any indication in Scripture that Paul ever was able to go to Spain. Some traditions hold that Paul eventually became a martyr in Rome. If you were to ask Paul, his mission was complete.

Chapter Sixteen

We must not read quickly over this chapter as it is easy to do with many of the lists in the Bible. We all have done it; we start reading the book of Matthew, just to jump past the list in the first half of chapter one that most like me won't remember anyway. Or maybe a bit more intriguing, but still seemingly useless, the list of all the men and their families who returned to Jerusalem with Zerubbabel in Ezra two. But the list here in Romans sixteen is very different. This is not just a list of people; these are people who were instrumental in the ministry of Paul. They made such an impact that Paul wanted the church to give special note to these names and give honor where honor was due. After these amazing acknowledgments, Paul is going to give us some closing thoughts.

I commend to you our sister Phoebe, a deacon of the church in Cenchreae. I ask you to receive her in the Lord in a way worthy of His people and to give her any help she may need from you, for she has been the benefactor of many people, including me. Greet Priscilla and Aquila, my co-workers in Christ Jesus. They risked their lives for me. Not only I but all the churches of the Gentiles are grateful to them. Greet also the church that meets at their house. Greet my dear friend Epenetus, who was the first convert to Christ in the province of Asia. Greet Mary, who worked very hard for you. Greet Andronicus and Junia, my fellow Jews who have been in prison with me. They are outstanding among the apostles, and they were in Christ before I was. Greet Ampliatus, my dear friend in the Lord. Greet Urbanus, our co-worker in Christ, and my dear friend Stachys. Greet Apelles, whose fidelity to Christ has stood the test. Greet those who belong to the household of Aristobulus. Greet Herodion, my fellow Jew. Greet those in the household of Narcissus who are in the Lord. Greet Tryphena and Tryphosa, those women who work hard in the Lord. Greet my dear friend Persis, another woman who has worked very hard in the Lord. Greet Rufus, chosen in the Lord, and his mother, who has been a mother to me, too. Greet Asyncritus, Phlegon, Hermes, Patrobas, Hermas and the other brothers and sisters with them. Greet Philologus, Julia, Nereus and his sister, and Olympas and all the Lord's people who are with them (Rom 16:1–15).

Phoebe—a deacon

The first of these special people in Paul's life was a woman named Phoebe, who was a deacon in the church in

Cenchreae. We need to be careful not to get caught up and distracted with conclusions about her being called a deacon. Some might presume she meets the qualifications of the *office* of a deacon laid out by Paul in his letter to Timothy. Some will argue against that, and say she was merely a *servant* in the church. I would like to stay away from a debate and agree that this woman, in whatever capacity and with or without a title, served in various ways for the enrichment of the kingdom.

Cenchreae was an eastern port of Corinth. Paul journeyed to Corinth twice; once on his second journey and finally on his third. This was one of the ports Paul likely would have used as he sailed out of that region. As I laid out in the introduction, Paul wrote this letter while he was in Corinth for three months on his third journey. As the three months had ended, Paul planned to head back to Jerusalem and deliver the contribution he raised for the church in Jerusalem. As Paul left Corinth, it was likely that he gave the letter intended for the church in Rome, this letter, to the care of Phoebe to deliver in person. As Paul headed toward Jerusalem, Phoebe headed toward Rome. Not exactly as planned, they would reconnect, but not in a few months, but in a few years.

Aquila and Priscilla

Paul met this wonderful couple while he was in Corinth (Acts 18), about 5–6 years prior to writing this letter. Paul was on his second journey, placing this meeting late 50–51 or 51–52 AD. Aquila and Priscilla were in Corinth due to the Jews being expelled from Rome in 49 AD. However, the edict ended between 54–57, allowing the Jews to return. It seems evident that Aquila and Priscilla took this opportunity to return to their home church in Rome. They were probably back in their home church for a couple of years when they received this letter from Paul at the hands of Phoebe. Paul praised Aquila and Priscilla for their hard work and even risking their lives for him. Paul also acknowledged the gathering that took place in their home. This was a very special relationship for Paul.

Epenetus

The first fruit of Asia. This is the same to say Epenetus was one of the first converts in that region. The King James Version (KJV), among a minority of other Bible translations, replaces Asia with Achaia. This is surprising since the Latin Vulgate, which the KJV relied heavily upon, uses *Asias* (Asia). Furthermore, When Paul wrote to Corinth, he spoke of the first converts in *Achaia*; the household of Stephanus (1 Cor 16:15). The first fruits of Asia would have been during Paul's first mission trip, while it was on Paul's second and third trip that he went into Achaia. Epenetus would have become a Christian sometime around 47–48 AD when Paul and Barnabas made a journey into Asia Minor. It seems evident that Epenetus not only surrendered his life to Christ but found his place in serving the church. When Paul wrote this letter to Rome, Epenetus was also there helping Aquila and Priscilla.

Mary

When we read this name, many of us probably wonder if this was one of the Marys in the stories of Christ, or perhaps His mother. But we simply do not know and are left only with speculation. Mary was a common name and could have easily been any Mary that worked hard at the church in Rome. Paul gave attention to her for all of her hard work.

Andronicus and Junia

Some believe these two Jews were fellow workers in Jerusalem. Perhaps they worked with Peter, James, and the other apostles. Paul noted that these two became Christians before he did, meaning they likely were hunted by Paul when he was Saul before he was a Christian and was persecuting the church. It seems ironic that they would all share a jail cell together for their faith in Christ. Andronicus and Junia were now working in the church in Rome.

Twenty names and two families

The many more names are not going to be listed individually, but that does not mean they were any less important to Paul. We just do not know much about them besides the passing phrase given by Paul. We do know that they played a special role in the ministry of Paul. Each of these workers found their place in the church in Rome. The other saints at the church in Rome may have not known the hard work of any of the above names. But Paul thought their contribution was important enough to make note of and give praise. By way of a last thought, I want to point out that Rufus could have been the son of Simon, the man who was forced to carry the cross of Christ (Mark 15:21). Again, it is only speculation, but the timeline fits. That would be one incredible story to tell.

> Greet one another with a holy kiss. All the churches of Christ send greetings (Rom 16:16).

As Paul brought the letter to a close, he made this comment that stirred a lot of debate over the years. It is likely and seems fitting that this form of greeting was an innocent kiss on the cheek, such as we see Judas giving Jesus in the garden, although the kiss of Judas was not so innocent. I was born and raised in the 21st-century American culture, by which this greeting is peculiar. However, many cultures, such as Latin America, still practice similar greetings of kissing on the cheek. I believe this greeting can be adapted to cultural changes. The point was not that we must *kiss* one another; Paul was urging the Christians to *greet* one another —acknowledge and encourage one another.

The Northern American cultural adaptation to this verse would be the shaking of hands. Perhaps a hug for some. The emphasis of Paul was the fellowship. I think it would bewilder Paul to see someone walk into church and leave right after without greeting anyone. This would be foreign to what Paul considered the body of Christ. Paul might even wonder if that person was a part of the *family*, the church.

> I urge you, brothers and sisters, to watch out for those who cause divisions and put obstacles in your way that are contrary to the teaching you have learned. Keep away from them. For such people are not serving our Lord

Christ, but their own appetites. By smooth talk and flattery they deceive the minds of naive people. Everyone has heard about your obedience, so I rejoice because of you; but I want you to be wise about what is good, and innocent about what is evil. The God of peace will soon crush Satan under your feet. The grace of our Lord Jesus be with you (Rom 16:17–20).

A large part of the letter to the church in Rome was to ensure that there was unity between the Gentile Christians and the Jewish Christians. This would have been important to Paul after having worked with the churches in Galatia where false teachers were attempting to Judaize the church. Many of the Christians in the church in Rome had recently spent some time in or around Asia Minor and Galatia, so they would have been quite aware of the false teachings. This simple exhortation by Paul would carry a strong message with it—Watch out! The wolves are out there.

Timothy, my co-worker, sends his greetings to you, as do Lucius, Jason and Sosipater, my fellow Jews. I, Tertius, who wrote down this letter, greet you in the Lord. Gaius, whose hospitality I and the whole church here enjoy, sends you his greetings. Erastus, who is the city's director of public works, and our brother Quartus send you their greetings. May the grace of our Lord Jesus Christ be with all of you. Amen (Rom 16:21–24).

Many of the members of the church in Rome had worked with Paul in Asia, Greece, and surrounding areas. Therefore, it would be expected that a good number of them would have known Timothy and some of the others that worked with Paul. Paul was being very relational and kept the church connected even while in different parts of the world.

Tertius would be considered an Amanuensis (someone employed to write a letter on behalf of another). Paul was aged and traditionally his vision was poor. It is likely, out of necessity, that he had Tertius write this letter for him. Either way, it seems evident that Paul dictated the words as Tertius wrote the letter. This would not have been uncommon as it was seen in other letters as well: 2 Thessalonians 3:17; Galatians 6:11; Philemon 19–20.

> Now to Him who is able to establish you in accordance with my gospel, the message I proclaim about Jesus Christ, in keeping with the revelation of the mystery hidden for long ages past, but now revealed and made known through the prophetic writings by the command of the eternal God, so that all the Gentiles might come to the obedience that comes from faith—to the only wise God be glory forever through Jesus Christ! Amen (Rom 16:25–27).

I want us to realize what Paul was saying in these last few verses. Remember that a primary message, which Paul called *good news* (gospel), was the inclusion of the Gentiles, the *full* inclusion of all of Israel. Paul said that this was all possible through God. Paul wanted them to rely on the establishing power of God to unite them in one faith in Jesus Christ.

Paul spoke of the *mystery of the gospel* several times when he wrote to the Ephesians. It seems clear that he was speaking of the plan of God to include the Gentiles in the grand plan of redemption. This was a mystery to many during that day. Salvation and the blessings of God were thought to be for the Jews, God's chosen people. The mystery that Paul was revealing was that God, being rich in mercy, was offering salvation to every person who takes a breath. God truly did send His Son to save the whole world.

—To the only wise God be glory forever through Jesus Christ! Amen.

Epilogue

I am using this space to attempt to draw a few key thoughts out. The letter written to the church in Rome is not a short letter. Furthermore, Paul packed it so full of rich gems useful to the early church, and not any less useful for the church now. What is a key message I believe can be taken from this letter? Salvation is for *all* and is through Christ. What a beautiful message. What greater message can ever be written? Who better could write this message than Paul, the one who spent the first half of his career persecuting the church and even killing Christians? The message not only on the scroll but from the depths of Paul's being was, *salvation is for even the worst of us*. There is no person outside of the reach of the love of God. People can travel as far from God in their sin, yet will find infinite love, while God waits with open arms for them to respond.

I want to leave two messages with you in closing. First, for my fellow Christians, your salvation is through Christ and His goodness—never forget that. But now that you have known the love of God, the world will never know unless you tell them; you too can be a part of this ministry of Paul to share the good news of Christ. The final message, if you are not a Christian, I commend you for traveling through this book. You have read, not just my book but one of the most amazing letters and books in the Bible. What I want you to know and never forget is that God loves you and wants to give you such amazing blessings, the greatest of them is salvation in Jesus Christ.

Scripture Index

Hebrews

1:3	80
9:16	66
10	53
11:17–19	40

James

2:20–24	37–38

1 Peter

1:17	114
1:19–20	48
1:20	52
2:24	44
4:3	148
5:8	148

2 Peter

3:9	136

Revelation

3:2	147
4	78

About the Author

My name is Brian Poe and I am married to Jesse Poe. I have two boys; Caleb is nine, and Benjamin is seven. I first began preaching for the Bad Axe Church of Christ in 2014. In late 2015, I moved back to the city where I began preaching for the Northeast Church of Christ. From there, I began preaching for the Dexter Church of Christ from 2018 to 2021. During this time, I also was pursuing my Masters of Divinity through Heritage Christian University. I obtained my MDiv in 2020 and soon later began my degree in Family Therapy through Amridge University. In 2021, I shifted my ministry focus and was accepted into a chaplain residency program at Covenant Healthcare. I finished my residency September in 2022. In the first part of 2023, I became the minister at the Escanaba Church of Christ in the Upper Peninsula of Michigan. I have loved to write and was able to publish my first book early in 2021 and my second in 2022. My goal from here is to continue to write as I minister in the church.

Also by Brian Poe

Who do you say I am?: a practical and relevant reflection of the life of Christ (2021)

The Magnitude of God: Exploring the Divine (2022)

Also by Cypress Publications

Always Near: Listening for Lessons from God
by Bill Bagents

The Christian Life: Chapters for Bible Teacher
by Ed Gallagher

Cruciform Christ: 52 Reflections on the Gospel of Mark
by Travis Bookout

Easing Life's Hurts 2nd ed.
by Jack Wilhelm and Bill Bagents

Equipping the Saints: A Practical Study of Ephesians 4:11–16
by Bill Bagents and Cory Collins

The Holy Spirit: A Bible Study Guide
by Jack Wilhelm

Jesus the Christ: Chapters for Bible Teachers
by Ed Gallagher

King of Glory: 52 Reflections on the Gospel of John
by Travis Bookout

The Magnitude of God

by Brian Poe

Rescue: God and Sin in the Old Testament
by John F. Wakefield

Revisiting Life's Oases: Soul-Soothing Stories
by Bill Bagents

Welcoming God's Word: Reading with Head and Heart
by Bill Bagents

WHAM! Facing Life's Heavy Hits: Thirteen Old Testament Encounters
by Bill and Laura S. Bagents

WHAM! Facing Life's Heavy Hits: Thirteen New Testament Encounters
by Bill and Laura S. Bagents

Women in the Shadows
by Betty Hamblen

CYPRESS

To see full catalog of Heritage Christian University Press
and its imprint Cypress Publications, visit
www.hcu.edu/publications